TAKING GOD SERIOUSLY

Are You Serious?

Ferdinand G. Mahfood
with Louise Perrotta

Food For The Poor, Inc.
550 SW 12th Avenue
Deerfield Beach, Florida 33442
www.foodforthepoor.org

Design by Marcia Montague
Photos by Gina Fontana
Back cover photo by Arne Roslund

Printed in the United States of America

CONTENTS

ACKNOWLEDGEMENTS

Grateful acknowledgement is made for permission to reprint copyrighted material:

From *The Cost of Discipleship* by Dietrich Bonhoeffer, translated from the German by R.H. Fuller, with some revision by Irmgard Booth. Copyright (c) 1959 by SCM Press, Ltd. Reprinted with the permission of SCM Press and Simon & Schuster.

From *The Confessions by St. Augustine.* Copyright (c) 1997 Augustinian Heritage Institute. Used by permission of the Augustinian Heritage Institute and New City Press.

From *Introduction to the Devout Life by St. Francis de Sales.* Copyright (c) 1950 by Harper & Brothers. Used by permission of Doubleday, a Division of Bantam Doubleday Dell Publishing Group, Inc.

From *Conjectures of a Guilty Bystander* by Thomas Merton. Copyright (c) 1966 by The Abbey of Gethsemani. Used by permission of Doubleday, a division of Bantam Doubleday Dell Publishing Group, Inc.

From *The Jesus I Never Knew* by Philip Yancey. Copyright (c) 1995 by Philip Yancey. Used by permission of Zondervan Publishing House.

From *The Christian Mind* by Harry Blamires. Copyright (c) 1963 by Harry Blamires. Published by Servant Publications, Ann Arbor, Michigan. Used with permission.

From *A Crisis of Truth* by Ralph Martin. Copyright (c) 1982 by Ralph Martin. Used with permission.

From *Tramp for the Lord* by Corrie ten Boom. Copyright (c) 1974 by Corri ten Boom and Jamie Buckingham. Used by permission of Fleming H. Revell, a division of Baker Book House Company.

The Myth of "Minimum Requirements" Christianity

What does it mean to be a follower of Jesus Christ?

There was a time when I believed that being a faithful Christian simply meant going to church on Sunday and trying not to break any of the Ten Commandments during the rest of the week. I was comfortable in my faith because I felt I was fulfilling my obligations. I lived and let live. Occasionally I even gave to the poor.

Eventually the routines that I called Christianity lulled me into a false sense that I was serious about God and that I had achieved what God wanted. Even though I had made some big mistakes in my life, I wasn't too concerned. It seemed to me that God lived far away in outer space on a big platform built by angels. How could this remote God be interested in the way I lived? Besides, I considered myself a basically good person. All I needed to do was wait for my turn to go to heaven on a rocket.

In some ways the fact that I felt so comfortable in my religious routines should have been a warning sign to me. My relationship with God was distant, casual, centered on what I wanted out of life. I wasn't God's servant; he was mine. And the way I lived showed it.

Then in January of 1976, as I was flying to Chicago on business, my complacent little world was changed forever. I had brought a book by Catherine Marshall, a Christmas present from my wife. While I was reading it, God broke into my consciousness and flooded me with an experience of love and mercy that I cannot possibly describe. I was blown apart. The Ferdinand Mahfood who got off that plane in Chicago wasn't the same man who had boarded it in Fort Lauderdale. And he has never been the same since.

Encountering God that day reoriented my whole life. It made me realize how unseriously I had been taking God. It began a process of healing and conversion that continues to this day. Eventually it led to the founding of Food For The Poor, through which you and I are helping to meet the material needs of some members of God's family who lack life's basic necessities.

So what does it mean to be a real follower of Jesus Christ? I now believe that it starts with a commitment to take God seriously—to live a life of service as Jesus did, to choose the rough and narrow road, to actively and regularly seek God's will above all else.

I know from experience how hard it is to accept this Gospel message. Perhaps that's because its very essence is tied to repentance, sacrifice, and action. Too often we're like the rich young man who came running to Jesus in search of eternal life (see Mark 10:17-22). His face fell when Jesus told him to sell all he had, give to the poor, and follow him along the hard road. Like that young man, we too resist dramatic change, especially when it jars us out of our comfortable lifestyle and leads us into the unknown.

Was the rich young man a bad person? Apparently not. He kept the commandments. But I suspect that he was playing games with his religion. He really wasn't open to moving beyond his usual religious observances and following Jesus down the road of sacrifice and service. The man recognized Jesus as "Teacher." But Jesus challenged his level of commitment by asking him, "Do you really take me seriously?"

Jesus asks each of us this question today. And I believe that how we answer is crucial—not just for ourselves but for many more people than we might think. God wants to catch our attention and bring us to a deeper level of joyful, unconditional love and service. For us too it's time to stop playing games.

In this series of books, collectively titled *Taking God Seriously*, I want to explore God's call to a radical and holy life. *Are You Serious?* begins the journey with a fundamental question that focuses attention on the very foundation of faith—our relationship with God. The booklet highlights some passages from Scripture, as well as related excerpts from the writings of some authors I respect. Future books will explore other subjects in the same way.

You'll notice that the excerpts in this series come from Christians of various denominations. I was raised a Catholic, and after my conversion I naturally turned first to the Catholic resources with which I was familiar. However, it didn't take long to discover the riches of other Christian traditions. This book reflects that discovery and is written for all who are interested in taking God seriously.

I invite you to read *Are You Serious?* slowly and thoughtfully. You might want to use it during your private prayer time. Or you could read and discuss it with another person or as part of a group. The reflection questions and prayer that follow each short section are intended as practical help in pursuing your conversation with God.

For me, taking God seriously began with a dramatic conversion. I know that's not the case for everyone. But I also know that serious discipleship doesn't depend on this kind of experience. The call to holiness and wholehearted love of God and neighbor is universal. All Christians, whether dramatically converted or not, are called to intimacy with God. Each of us is to "be perfect," as our heavenly Father is perfect (Matthew 5:48). Being a "good enough" Christian who coasts along with the crowd just isn't good enough!

Of course this call would be daunting if we had to respond on our own. But the good news is that God makes it possible. If we let him, God will change us from "nice" people into "new" ones, as C.S. Lewis put it—into men and women who, by the power of Jesus living in us, can obey the command to be perfect.

I offer these reflections in the sincere hope that they will encourage you or someone you know to follow Jesus more closely. May God's great love draw you as you consider his call and your response to that all-important question, "Are you serious?"

Ferdinand Mahfood

Games Christians Play

The word of Jesus demands action,

which means not just doing things,

but a certain response to a call.

It means a "yes"…

God will not be mocked.

To play with his things is

literally to play with fire.

Jean Vanier

The Not-So-Rich Young Man

s he was setting out on a journey, a man ran up and knelt before him, and asked him, "Good Teacher, what must I do to inherit eternal life?" Jesus said to him, "Why do you call me good? No one is good but God alone. You know the commandments: 'You shall not murder; You shall not commit adultery; You shall not steal; You shall not bear false witness; You shall not defraud; Honor your father and mother.'" He said to him, "Teacher, I have kept all these since my youth." Jesus, looking at him, loved him and said, "You lack one thing: go, sell what you own, and give the money to the poor, and you will have treasure in heaven; then come, follow me." When he heard this, he was shocked and went away grieving, for he had many possessions.

Mark 10:17-22

You have to hand it to this man. Whatever his faults, he was clear about life's most important question and put it to Jesus right away. But how sincere was he?

I suggest that what he wanted from Jesus was an opinion, something he could choose to follow or not, rather than a divine command to "follow me." Maybe he prided himself on the way he had kept the commandments. Certainly he considered himself a God-fearing, law-abiding person. "I'm already doing every-thing right," he seemed to think.

Yet when Jesus put him to the test, this man showed himself incapable of the single-minded obedience God expects. He was too attached to his riches to attach himself to Jesus.

I think that many of us today, even well-intentioned Christians and religious professionals, are in this game-playing business. That's one of the reasons the world is in the shape it's in. We come to Jesus for comfort or encouragement or even advice, but we don't want any commands! Unconditionally putting ourselves and all our possessions into God's hands—that's just too scary, we think. And far too demanding. We shrink from the challenge.

According to Thomas Merton, the laziness and cowardice that feed this game-playing mentality are two of the greatest enemies of real discipleship. They make our comfort the first priority; they look to the material world and not God for security. "But sooner or later, if we follow Christ," says Merton, "we have to risk everything in order to gain everything. We have to gamble on the invisible and risk all that we can see and taste and feel."

This means being willing to surrender all we have—our money, time, talents, and our very selves—and admit how poor we are before God no matter how many such riches we possess. The Bible devotes a great deal of attention to the poor. The Old Testament shows that the oppression of weak and defenseless people rouses God's anger. In a surprising development, though, Jesus also singles out the poor as "blessed."

"Blessed are you who are poor, for yours is the kingdom of heaven" (Luke 6:20). Why would Jesus say that a person who is poor has a spiritual edge over the one who is rich?

From my many encounters with desperately poor people throughout the Caribbean, I think it's because they know how much they need help! They have no riches to give them a false sense of security. They aren't necessarily virtuous, but they are less likely than many of us to pretend that they are. When they turn to God for help, they aren't playing games: they are serious! And they are ready to do whatever God asks.

That's why I have no doubt that many of these people are really the rich ones among us. I think of 80-year-old Nellie—blind, hunchbacked, living in a bleak shelter in Haiti. I used to visit her, sit on her bed, give her a hug, and laugh with her.

"Nellie, I want to bring you a present," I told her one day. Her answer wasn't what I expected. "My friend, what could I possibly want? I already have everything." Nellie was destitute, blind, crippled, and often in pain, but she was very close to Jesus. Materially she had nothing; spiritually she had everything.

Taking God seriously means imitating the poverty of people like Nellie. Not that we should necessarily sell all and move into the slums. But we should be so detached from what we have that if God asked us to do this or anything else, we would.

Otherwise, we are like that not-so-rich, game-playing young man—not ready for God's kingdom, not ready to obey and follow Jesus wherever He leads.

Making it real

Slowly reread the story of
the rich young man.
(You might want to look up
the parallel accounts in
Matthew 19:16-20 and Luke 18:18-30.)

What do you think his problem was?

Do you think he noticed how
Jesus looked at him?

Ask yourself: What are my riches?

Is there any attachment that is preventing
me from responding to Jesus' look of love?

Giving it to God

Jesus, how foolish I am sometimes!
Forgive me for clinging to "riches"
that only impoverish me.

What could possibly compare
with being loved by you?

NOTES:

The Game of "Yes, but..."

I f, as we read our Bibles, we heard Jesus speaking to us in this way today [as he spoke to the rich young man], we should probably try to argue ourselves out of it like this: "It is true that the demand of Jesus is definite enough, but I have to remember that he never expects us to take his commands legalistically. What he really wants me to have is faith. But my faith is not necessarily tied up with riches or poverty or anything of the kind..."

How is such absurdity possible? What has happened that the word of Jesus can be thus degraded by this trifling, and thus left open to the mockery of the world? When orders are issued in other spheres of life there is no doubt whatever of their meaning. If a father sends his child to bed, the boy knows at once what he has to do. But suppose he has picked up a smattering of pseudo-theology. In that case he would argue more or less like this: "Father tells me to go to bed, but he really means that I am tired, and he does not want me to be tired. I can overcome my tiredness just as well if I go out and play. Therefore, though father tells me to go to bed, he really means: 'Go out and play.'" If a child tried such arguments on his father or a citizen on his government, they would both meet with a kind of language they could not fail to understand—in short, they would be punished. Are we to treat the commandment of Jesus differently from other orders and exchange single-minded obedience for downright disobedience? How could that be possible?

Dietrich Bonhoeffer

"Jesus couldn't possibly have meant that" is the name of this game. In it, perfectly clear commands and statements are downplayed and reinterpreted to mean something quite different from what Jesus intended. Dietrich Bonhoeffer, a Lutheran pastor in Germany who defied the Nazis and was executed for it, refused to play this game.

I think that many of us do play this game, but without realizing it fully. Maybe we have never understood (or wanted to understand) that the Gospel is radical. Instead of letting it challenge us, we unthinkingly accept a watered-down version (presented sometimes even from the pulpit). Or somewhere along the way we learn that Jesus used exaggeration to make a point: "hate your father and mother," he said, "tear out your eye" (Luke 14:26; Mark 9:47). We know that these are figures of speech and not to be taken literally. But then we wrongly assume that this is the way to interpret every command in the Bible. As Bonhoeffer points out, this leads to fuzzy thinking and downright disobedience.

"Do not worry" (Matthew 6:25). We all know that every responsible person worries. Jesus just meant that I shouldn't sweat the small stuff.

"Forgive others their trespasses" (Matthew 6:14). Obviously Jesus wasn't talking about really serious offenses, like what my business partner just did to me.

"Do not store up for yourselves treasures on earth" (Matthew 6:19). It doesn't really matter how much money I make as long as I don't act stuck-up and I realize that I can't take it with me.

From my own experience I am very familiar with this game of limiting the meaning of Jesus' words. I also have been very good at the closely related game of limiting their scope. That is to say, I have been a one-day-a-week Christian. God and his word were for Sundays only. And what I heard or did in church had no impact on the rest of my life.

Another German pastor, Helmut Thielicke, gave a good description of people who hang around Jesus in this half-hearted way. They travel a double track: "On Sundays they are glad to attend a service and listen to a sermon. They may even be stirred by it momentarily. But as soon as they are back at the shop, the machine, or the office on Monday, it is as if they had turned a switch."

To do this is to relate to the church as a filling station. We attend the liturgy, hear a sermon, and maybe receive the Eucharist. Then we go home and watch TV and drink beer and never think about God again. The next Sunday we repeat the same routine— and on and on for our whole existence. Our worship of God should be transforming, informing, and invigorating every aspect of life. Tragically, we miss it.

We can't limit Jesus' words to us without also limiting—even losing—our own happiness. Single-minded obedience is the only effective response to our Lord's commands.

Making it real

Do I ever reinterpret Scripture
to suit myself?

What do I think of Bonhoeffer's statement
that this is "downright disobedience"?

Do I have a "filling station"
approach to church?

What could I do to be more
focused on Jesus wherever I am,
whatever I do this week?

Giving it to God

Sometimes we're no different
from the roach and the cricket!
They pass beside the Bible
and even eat at its pages,
but don't practice its teachings.

Prayer of a Haitian Christian

Jesus, am I like that sometimes?

Help me to love your word and
live it fully in every area of my life.
I don't want to be a
"yes, but" Sunday Christian!

NOTES:

Delayed Reaction

ne of the things I most admire about Augustine is his burning love for God. I particularly appreciate his honesty about the games he played to avoid taking God seriously.

By the time he was converted in 386, Augustine had managed to dodge God for more than a decade. "I had been putting off the moment, when by spurning earthly happiness, I would clear space in my life to search for wisdom," he admits regretfully in his Confessions. "Twelve years, perhaps, had gone to waste, and I with them."

For Augustine one big obstacle to real discipleship was his unwillingness to follow Christ's teaching about sexual relationships. "Grant me chastity and self-control, but please not yet," he used to pray. Afraid that God might immediately hear and heal him of the out-of-control desires which he was "more anxious to satisfy than to snuff out," he kept delaying the moment of repentance.

Augustine's misery over his double-mindedness came to a head one afternoon in a garden in Milan. His account of how God's grace and mercy broke into his life includes this gripping description of his struggle to put game-playing aside.

"Let it be now," I was saying to myself. "Now is the moment, let it be now," and merely by saying this I was moving toward the decision. I would almost achieve it, but then fall just short...I shrank from dying to death and living to life, for ingrained evil was more powerful in me than new-grafted good. The nearer it came, that moment when I would be changed, the more it pierced me with terror. Dismayed, but not quite dislodged, I was left hanging.

The frivolity of frivolous aims, the futility of futile pursuits, these things that had been my cronies of long standing, still held me back, plucking softly at my garment of flesh and murmuring in my ear, "Do you mean to get rid of us? Shall we never be your companions again after that moment ... never ... never again? From that time onward so-and-so will be forbidden to you, all your life long..."

But now their voices were less than half as loud, for they no longer confronted me directly to argue their case, but muttered behind my back and slyly tweaked me as I walked away, trying to make me look back. Yet they did slow me down, for I could not bring myself to tear free and shake them off and leap across to that place whither I was summoned, while aggressive habit still taunted me: "Do you imagine you will be able to live without these things?"

Augustine of Hippo

I don't know about you, but I find it encouraging that God doesn't hold our delaying tactics against us. When we get to the point of wanting Him more than we want anything else, He is there to welcome us.

Maybe one reason Augustine's story hits home with me is that for a long time I held God at arm's length too. I was in my forties when I was converted during that plane ride. I was totally self-centered and focused on my comforts and pleasures.

Today I wonder how I could have been so blind to the fact that God is the only reality and the only reason for living. Now that I have tasted God, it puzzles me that anything else could ever have attracted me more. With Augustine all I can do is tell God how sorry I am to have kept him waiting. "Late have I loved you, Beauty so ancient and so new, late have I loved you! Lo, you were within, but I outside, seeking there for you."

What frightens me is that it is possible to play ring around the rosy or hide and seek with God for a lifetime. Many people do. They fritter away all their days in distractions—running around this earth like chickens with their heads chopped off, busy with all sorts of things and missing the only thing necessary. And as with Augustine, the longer we postpone turning to God, the more ingrained and stubborn our sins and bad habits become.

I think we need a sense of urgency about taking God seriously—and about continuing to take him seriously every step of the way. "Now is the acceptable time," Scripture tells us, "now is the day of salvation" (2 Corinthians 6:2).

No matter where we are in our relationship with Jesus, today is the day of salvation for us. Let's not miss whatever grace of conversion God is offering.

Making it real

How often have I played the game of
"give me grace, God—but not yet"?
Is there any area in which
I'm playing it now?

Have I ever been envious of people who
had genuine deathbed conversions?
("They got to have their cake and eat it too.")

Am I convinced that turning to Jesus as fast
as possible is always the best decision?

Giving it to God

Take, O Lord,
and receive my entire liberty,
my memory, my understanding,
and my whole will.
All that I am, all that I have,
you have given me,
and I will give it back to you.

Ignatius Loyola

Lord, give me the grace to pray and
keep praying this prayer sincerely.
Let it be now!

NOTES:

Phantoms of Devotion

 veryone paints devotion according to his own passions and fancies. A man given to fasting thinks himself very devout if he fasts, although his heart may be filled with hatred. Much concerned with sobriety, he doesn't dare to wet his tongue with wine or even water, but won't hesitate to drink deep of his neighbor's blood by detraction and calumny. Another man thinks himself devout because he daily recites a vast number of prayers, but after saying them he utters the most disagreeable, arrogant, and harmful words at home and among the neighbors. Another gladly takes a coin out of his purse and gives it to the poor, but he cannot extract kindness from his heart and forgive his enemies. Another forgives his enemies but never pays his creditors unless compelled to do so by force of law. All these men are usually considered to be devout, but they are by no means such...

Many persons clothe themselves with certain outward actions connected with holy devotion, and the world believes that they are truly devout and spiritual, whereas they are in fact nothing but copies and phantoms of devotion.

Francis de Sales

What keeps us from taking God seriously? One obstacle—perhaps our greatest, judging from the number of times Jesus denounced it—is hypocrisy. For sure, this is a temptation we must overcome again and again in our walk with the Lord.

Hypocrites look like they are worshiping God, but in reality it is themselves they are putting forward. Remember the Pharisee who was praying in the temple (Luke 18:9-14)? "God, I thank you that I am not like other people," he began. Then he listed reasons why God should consider him superior to, say, that poor tax collector in the back.

Most people who knew him would have agreed with the Pharisee's self-assessment. He looked good. His outward piety was impeccable. But God, who sees the heart, was not impressed. What good are religious observances that don't express a person's obedience to the great commandment? "You shall love the Lord your God with all your heart, and with all your soul, and with all your mind" (Matthew 22:37). The Pharisee was too full of self-love to focus on God. He brimmed over with pride at his gifts and achievements. Fixated on his own worth, he mentally downgraded the tax collector and also violated the second great commandment: "You shall love your neighbor as yourself" (Matthew 22:39).

One reason Jesus was so severe with those scribes and Pharisees who were hypocritical is that, as the religious leaders, they were supposed to be leading people to God yet were failing to do so. Some of them were not only proud but greedy (see Luke 20:45-47). Now, I'm not a religious leader and probably you aren't either. But that doesn't let us off the hook! There's probably a bit of the Pharisee in each of us.

Many Christians play the game of looking good. Social pressure and the desire for admiration lead to religious practice that is only skin deep and not from the heart. Some of us relate to the church as a secular organization, with rules and rewards to pursue, where we climb the rungs to greater recognition. We may feel virtuous. We may even be applauded. But meanwhile, we lose sight of the Lord.

In time we come to believe in our own righteousness. Even if we don't put it in words, our whole attitude says to God: "Hey, look at me! I'm a pretty good person. Look at all I've done for you. You're pretty lucky to have such a talented disciple."

How could we so easily forget that everything we have comes from God? All our talents, our material goods, our relationships, our time, our very bodies— everything flows from God. He is the only reality! And He is behind any degree of success that we experience.

God help me if I ever start thinking that Food For The Poor is my own doing. What did I know about helping the poor on that day 17 years ago when I called my accountant to see about setting up some sort of nonprofit corporation? I had no conception of what to do or how to do it. How can I account for the statistics? Millions of dollars' worth of goods shipped to the poor since we began; hundreds of thousands of people like you helping us to do it... How did it happen? It all emanated from God! I'm not that good!

The cure for hypocrisy is self-knowledge. The beginning of the spiritual life, someone once said, is to know who you are and to know who God is. That knowledge, which can only come from God, keeps things in perspective. Without it, we will set ourselves up as little gods, fashioning a religion in our own image, in which our own virtues shine out in comparison to other people's failures. Without self-knowledge, we will become the "phantoms of devotion" that Francis de Sales describes.

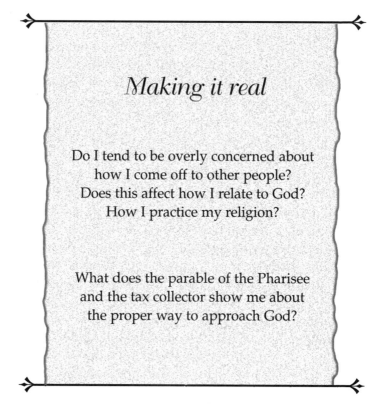

Making it real

Do I tend to be overly concerned about
how I come off to other people?
Does this affect how I relate to God?
How I practice my religion?

What does the parable of the Pharisee
and the tax collector show me about
the proper way to approach God?

Talking to God

Search me, O God,
and know my heart;
test me and know my thoughts.
See if there is any wicked way in me,
and lead me in the way everlasting.

Psalm 139:23-24

NOTES:

NOTES:

SECTION TWO

A God That Isn't God

God is greater than God.

Meister Eckhart

Who Are You, God?

 e still, and know that I am God!

I am exalted among the nations,

I am exalted in the earth.

Psalm 46:11

Usually when I think about this verse, I reflect on the first two words. They emphasize the need for quiet and calm in turning to God. But some time ago, the words "I am God" caught my attention.

"I am God." Who is God? What is He like? Serious God-seekers throughout the centuries have found some answers by reflecting on the complexity and magnificence of the universe and the human person that God has created. The Bible is the record of God's actions in history to reveal His love and power.

But this doesn't mean that we now know everything there is to know about God. Because our knowledge comes from God, it is sure; because we are mere creatures, it is also limited. This is why the Eastern liturgy refers to God as "the inexpressible, the incomprehensible, the invisible, the ungraspable."

Impossible for creatures to fully understand the Creator! Our words and ideas simply cannot encompass the reality that is God.

I like the way the medieval mystic, Meister Eckhart, put it: "God is greater than God." In other words, any conception of God we have will always be topped by who God actually is. Centuries before Eckhart another Christian writer cautioned that "if anyone, when he has seen God, understands what he has seen, it is never God that he has seen." And Thomas Merton, zeroing in on just one divine quality, observed that God is mercy within mercy within mercy — in other words, a mercy whose depths we cannot fathom.

It's important to be humble before this unfathomable God, to keep our limitations firmly in mind. Otherwise, we will consciously or unconsciously attempt to cut Him down to size. And once we relate to God as someone who can be tamed and controlled, He becomes a figment of our imagination—hardly someone to take seriously.

J.B. Phillips, a British theologian and Scripture scholar, once explored this problem in a book with the wonderful title, *Your God Is Too Small*. In it he contended that many people today have not found a God "big enough for modern needs." They have become very knowledgeable about many areas of life, but their ideas of God have remained at the Sunday-school level. Since their faith is based on an inadequate view of God, it is juvenile and unworkable for everyday life.

Phillips gives a very entertaining picture of some of the most popular "unreal" gods to which many Christians cling. In fact, I recognized my own pre-conversion view of God in some of these descriptions.

Because these distorted images are so deficient, Christians who have them will probably be tempted to worship other "gods" too. For myself, I can say that even though I attended nine o'clock Mass most Sundays, I was also worshiping at the altar of power, control, and self-esteem. Nobody calls such things "God," but as Phillips comments, "they have the influence and command the devotion which should belong to the real God."

In this chapter we will explore some of the false images which undermine the love and trust that God deserves. Maybe you too will recognize your "god" in some of these descriptions. If your relationship with God has become casual and predictable, as mine was, this chapter may provide some clues as to why: a failure to understand or appreciate God's awesomeness will inevitably dull and sidetrack anyone's spiritual life.

But God—the real God—has not left us orphans. If we turn to Him, He will correct our misimpressions and forgive our idol worshiping. He will reveal himself to us as He really is. And having tasted something of the living God, we will stand amazed.

Making it real

If someone were to ask me what
I think God is like, what would I say?

When was the last time I gave serious
thought to God's incomparable greatness?

What practical steps could I take to grow
into a more mature understanding of God?

Talking to God

I know you so little, dear God,
and so much of what I think I know
may be off the mark.
Give me the love and faith
to know you as you really are.

O the depth of the riches and wisdom
and knowledge of God!
How unsearchable are his judgments
and how inscrutable his ways!
"For who has known the mind of the Lord?
Or who has been his counselor?"
"Or who has given a gift to him,
to receive a gift in return?"
For from him and through him
and to him are all things.
To him be the glory forever.
Amen.

Romans 11:33-36

NOTES:

A Policeman and a Lollipop for Good Behavior

 great many Christians actually seem to think that all their Father in heaven wants is a chance to make them miserable and to take away all the blessings, and they imagine, poor souls, that if they hold on to things in their own will, they can hinder him from doing this. I am ashamed to write the words, and yet we must face a fact which is making wretched hundreds of lives.

A Christian lady who had this feeling was once expressing to a friend how impossible she found it to say, "Thy will be done," and how afraid she should be to do it. She was the mother of one little boy, who was the heir to a great fortune and the idol of her heart.

After she had stated her difficulties fully, her friend said, "Suppose your little Charley should come running to you tomorrow and say, "Mother, I have made up my mind to let you have your own way with me from this time forward. I am always going to obey you, and I want you to do just whatever you think best with me. I know you love me, and I am going to trust myself to your love." How would you feel towards him? Would you say to yourself, "Ah, now I shall have a chance to make Charley miserable. I will take away all his pleasures and fill his life with every hard and disagreeable thing I can find. I will compel him to do just the things that are the most difficult for him to do, and I will give him all sorts of impossible commands"?

"Oh no, no, no!" exclaimed the indignant mother. "You know I would not. You know I would hug him to my heart and cover him with kisses and would hasten to fill his life with all that was sweetest and best."

"And are you more tender and loving than God?" asked her friend.

Hannah Whitall Smith

Someone recently told me about a woman who became so convinced that God was out to get her that she stopped praying. Her "God" was always lying in wait to catch her out in a mistake. If she didn't know what to pray for or phrase her prayers exactly right, she worried, this cruel judge would punish her by giving her whatever mistaken or imperfect thing she had asked for. And he would enjoy watching her suffer the consequences.

Where does this twisted idea of God come from? Whatever the source, I agree with Hannah Whitall Smith that it makes many Christians miserable. Not all of them stop praying. But none of them can relate to God with the wholehearted trust that "little Charley" shows his mother.

What a terrible thing to turn God into a mean policeman! Religion becomes a mere legalistic exercise of staying out of jail. Go to church and fulfill your Sunday obligation; obey all the rules. Then when you die, you'll go to heaven.

Following Jesus does involve doing right and avoiding wrong. At the end of time Jesus will return as judge. But to cower before God as a stern prosecutor is to completely misunderstand who He is for us. To view this relationship as a "rules and future reward" proposition is to empty it of its true meaning.

That's not how Jesus talked about discipleship. Jesus said, "I came that they may have divine life, and have it abundantly" (John 10:10). We don't have to wait till after we die to find happiness. Divine life starts here! Heaven starts here! As Catherine of Siena said, "All the way to heaven is heaven, because Jesus said, 'I am the way.'"

Why did Jesus go to all the trouble of breaking into the human condition and sharing our life and death? It wasn't to hold out a lollipop, to dangle a promise of future reward if only we would keep his rules. Jesus lived among us, suffered, died, and rose so that we could begin experiencing His divine life here on this earth.

Perhaps because it took me so long to get it, this has become one of my favorite themes. J.B. Phillips underlined it too. Heaven is not "the reward for 'being a good boy,'" he explained; it is "the continuation and expansion of a quality of life which begins when a man's central confidence is transferred from himself to God-become-man." Phillips found it significant that Jesus spoke of eternal life "as being entered into now, though plainly to extend without limitation after the present incident that we call life." Whoever really believes what Jesus said already has that quality of eternal life, Phillips contended—"not merely 'life,' but life of a deeper and more enduring quality."

"Divine life to the full": no one who wants to take God seriously will want to miss the exciting implications of Jesus' promise.

Making it real

Does the "mean policeman"
view of God ring any bells for me?

If yes, can I tell where it comes from?

How closely does my image of God
correspond to Scripture's description
of the God who "so loved the world
that he gave his only Son"
(John 3:16)?

How would I complete the sentence,
"Heaven is ... "?

Would I include the word "now"
in my explanation?

Talking to God

Dear Father,
instead of offering you loving trust,
I so often relate to you in fearful,
suspicious ways.

Overcome my resistance with your love.
Fill me with your abundant life and
let me taste heaven here on earth.

NOTES:

No News, Good News

ny word that comes from God is news!

But our ideas of news, the newspapers' idea of news, might lead us to believe that any word except what came from God was news. As if what was said by God had to be so fixed, so determined, so rigid in its set form that it could never be anything new, never unpredictable, never astonishing, never frightening. If there is no risk in revelation, if there is no fear in it, if there is no challenge in it, if it is not a word which creates whole new worlds, and new beings, if it does not call into existence a new creature, our new self, then religion is dead and God is dead. Those for whom the Gospel is old, and old only, have killed it for the rest of men. The life of the Gospel is its newness.

Those who preach the Gospel as if it were not and could not be news, as if it could never be news again, are saying in their own way, and much more terribly than Nietzsche, that "God is dead." They are declaring it officially, they are proclaiming it not just as the paradox of an eccentric, but as the doctrine of their church.

What makes the Gospel news? The faith, which is created in us by God and with which we hear it as news.

Thomas Merton

"Boring" and "predictable" are two adjectives that many people, if they were honest, would use to describe their experience of God and Christianity. Look around many churches on a Sunday morning and you will catch the tell-tale indicators: glazed eyes, fidgets, distracted looks.

The pious bored (and I was among them) are going through the motions. They don't hear the Gospel as God's personal word to them. For them it is the "no news, no risk" message that Thomas Merton contrasts with the real thing. They are never surprised or fed or prodded along by it. If they receive communion, it doesn't cause them to fall madly in love with God or to go out and serve God's people. These Christians have boxed God into a tiny "churchy" corner where he can do no harm.

How has this happened? In some cases the gospel is stripped of excitement by treating it only as ancient tradition. It is not presented as both old and new— "new every morning," like God's mercies (Lamentations 3:23). Sometimes in our church life we let the Gospel become a dead letter, respectable and irrelevant.

Sometimes we produce a "no news" Gospel by seeking only words of comfort and affirmation. We want God to be a kind of Santa Claus, always ready to shower prosperity on his people. Never a disturbing word here, nothing to unsettle people's deep-seated assumptions about their "rights" to health, wealth, ease, and personal gratification. "I try not to talk about subjects that make people uncomfortable," one pastor told Charles Colson. "My job is to make sure that they will come back here week after week."

When we drop the language of Christ for the language of the culture, no wonder people lose interest. Where is the newness of the Gospel, when it is barely distinguishable from the messages of our society? People have heard it all before. They hear it every day from their TVs and radios and newspapers.

The message of the Gospel was profoundly disturbing and unsettling when it was first preached. It was so countercultural that people found it threatening, even offensive. Read Jesus' words carefully, and you will see that this is still true today. In his book *The Jesus I Never Knew*, Philip Yancey makes this point by contrasting the American Dream with the Beatitudes:

The Beatitudes express quite plainly that God views this world through a different set of lenses. God seems to prefer the poor and those who mourn to the Fortune 500 and supermodels who frolic on the beach. Oddly, God may prefer South Central L.A. to Malibu Beach, and Rwanda to Monte Carlo. In fact, one could almost subtitle the Sermon on the Mount not "survival of the fittest" but "triumph of the victims"....

Strength, good looks, connections, and the competitive instinct may bring a person success in a society like ours, but those very qualities may block entrance to the kingdom of heaven. Dependence, sorrow, repentance, a longing to change—these are the gates to God's kingdom.

At every turn Jesus upsets our preconceived ideas and reverses our expectations. He extends divine life, but only at the price of our own. He offers an easy yoke, but also a cross. He promises His followers bounty—"houses, brothers and sisters ... with persecutions" (Mark 10:30). The way to win is to lose. To be first, be last. Seek God in the poor. Take a place of service in this life and receive a place of honor in the next.

Challenging? Of course! Disturbing? Often. But never boring and predictable. Take Jesus seriously, and life will never be dull again.

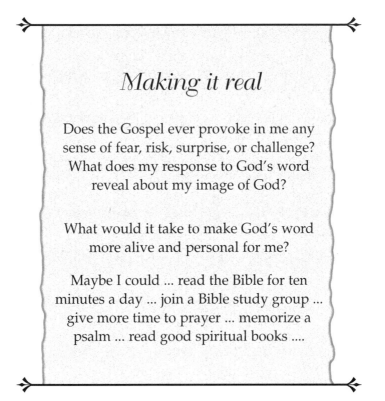

Making it real

Does the Gospel ever provoke in me any sense of fear, risk, surprise, or challenge? What does my response to God's word reveal about my image of God?

What would it take to make God's word more alive and personal for me?

Maybe I could ... read the Bible for ten minutes a day ... join a Bible study group ... give more time to prayer ... memorize a psalm ... read good spiritual books ....

Talking to God

Holy Spirit, you who make all things
new, bring Scripture to life for me.

May my heart be set on fire as you open
to me the wonders of your holy word!

NOTES:

Outer Space Deity

ne day when my grandson Matthew was five, I asked him, "Where is God?" He pointed to his heart. Four years later I asked him the same question. He pointed to the sky.

Like Matthew, most of us seem to have lost God. We have gotten the idea that he's up there and we're down here. But God isn't a remote figure sitting on a platform above the moon and stars, as I used to think. When Jesus ascended, he didn't go up into the air like a rocket. He entered into glory with the Father and, by his Spirit, he went into the human heart. God isn't in never-never land, but within.

Jesus told the disciples, "The kingdom of God is not coming with things that can be observed; nor will they say, "Look, here it is!" or "There it is!" For in fact, the kingdom of God is within you" (Luke 17:20-21). A popular spiritual writer imagines Jesus expanding on this point for his modern-day disciples:

You go on like children, searching for heaven near the moon or the stars. But to see it, feel it, live it, you must look within yourselves. I, the king, am within you, and together we form the reign of God, which is something that already exists, even if it has yet to be made visible and proclaimed to all creation...

But do you know why you are always making mistakes? Why you are always finding yourselves at the beginning again? Why you live in fear and constant lack of decision?

Because you do not believe in this reality. Because you take those words, I in you and you in Me, to be rhetorical, whereas they are the naked truth.

I am truly in you. I live in you, and you never realize it…

What offends Me most is your unbelief. You take the Gospel as a fairy tale, or nearly so. You do not believe what I have said. If you believed you would know that I am within you as a living reality, not a beautiful, sentimental phrase. If you believed that I am within you, if you acted on my words "Live on in my love," all your problems would be resolved, and you would be Christians who were a bit more serious and less strange.

Carlo Carretto

Each of us comes from God and is sustained by God. At every moment God is breathing life into us and keeping us in existence. If that were not the case, I wouldn't be writing this and you wouldn't be reading it. To be alive is to share in the life of the great "I am." "In him we live and move and have our being" (Acts 17:28). At every microsecond we are being brought forth by this Creator who is constantly creating.

God is Being to such a degree that we might almost say He is the only reality. He is my life, my soul, my sanity, the center of my consciousness. He is more me than I am me!

But so many of us haven't found this real self within. So many of us weren't taught or didn't develop the concept that we are not separate from God, that in Christ we are one with God. Where does this pervasive sense of separation come from?

Fundamentally, Scripture tells us, it came about because of a false idea about God. Adam and Eve listened to the serpent's insinuations and became convinced that God was holding out on them. Describing the fall from grace through which sin entered into the world, the Catholic Catechism observes that Adam and Eve became "afraid of the God of whom they conceived a distorted image—that of a God jealous of his prerogatives." A profound sense of distance from the Creator, passed along to the whole human race, is among the tragic consequences of our first parents' distrust and disobedience.

But our Father wants us to know that Jesus has overcome the separation of sin. Through the power of the Holy Spirit at work in His death and resurrection, Jesus reopened the way back to God. Sin's cosmic dimension is broken. We don't need to feel separated from God any longer.

Amazing the lengths to which God went to reach out to us. Amazing His plans for us now. What Jesus won for us goes far beyond simple reconciliation; it is the possibility of union with God. "As you, Father, are in me and I am in you, may they also be in us," Jesus prayed for all His disciples to come (John 17:21). And ever since, every disciple who takes this invitation seriously sets out on the road of conversion and repentance. So begins that mysterious process in which God gradually restructures our consciousness and brings us to the point where we can say with Jesus and in Jesus, "The Father and I are one."

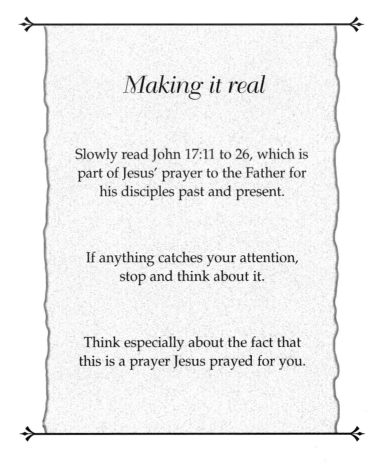

Making it real

Slowly read John 17:11 to 26, which is part of Jesus' prayer to the Father for his disciples past and present.

If anything catches your attention, stop and think about it.

Think especially about the fact that this is a prayer Jesus prayed for you.

Talking to God

As you, Father,
are in me and I am in you,
may they also be in us....
The glory that you have given me
I have given them,
so that they may be one,
as we are one,
I in them and you in me.

John 17:20, 22-23

Jesus, I join my prayer to yours.

NOTES:

NOTES:

Words of Life and Truth

Let's extinguish the devil's flaming arrows

while they are still a long way off,

knocking them down through

the constant reading of sacred Scripture.

For it is simply not possible

for anyone to be saved

who does not constantly

take advantage of spiritual reading!

John Chrysostom

Meeting Jesus in His Word

ndeed, the word of God is living and active, sharper than any two-edged sword, piercing until it divides soul from Spirit, joints from marrow; it is able to judge the thoughts and intentions of the heart. And before him no creature is hidden, but all are naked and laid bare to the eyes of the one to whom we must render an account.

Hebrews 4:12-13

For me, this description of Scripture's power to unveil the truth captures something of what it was like to encounter God on that Chicago-bound plane in 1976. One reason I could feel so loved by that experience was that I also felt so known. It was mind-boggling to realize that God saw every part of me, including all the dark corners, and that He loved me anyway—far beyond anything I could have imagined! I was truly "laid bare to the eyes of the one to whom we must render an account," but they were loving eyes. Under their gaze I began to be revealed to myself and to be transformed.

Searching out, revealing, transforming—this is what God's word does to us. Through the power of the Holy Spirit, the inspired word of God puts us in direct contact with Jesus, the living Word of God.

This contact, experienced on a regular basis, is fundamental for every follower of Christ. As the theologian J.I. Packer said, though discipleship can be described from many angles, the Christian is basically the person "who acknowledges and lives under the word of God."

Taking God seriously means taking His word seriously. Not that you read it in the impersonal way you'd read a computer manual or a cookbook or an introduction to German grammar. Taking Scripture seriously is not primarily a matter of learning the rules. Above all, it means coming to Scripture with expectancy and eagerness, a personal encounter with God. It means listening. It means being open and willing to do what God tells you, even if it turns your life upside down.

In this chapter we'll consider some aspects of God's word that tend to get downplayed or distorted today: the fact that it's objectively true, that it's knowable, that it requires a response, that it's not abstract but brings God into our everyday life.

I hope these reflections will encourage you to take stock of your own relationship with Scripture. If you are already taking it seriously, let them stimulate your efforts. If you have not really begun, consider this your personal invitation to plunge in and discover Jesus "living and active" in his word.

And lest anyone think that daily meditating on Scripture is something only for retirees or pastors, consider how the "golden-mouthed" preacher, John Chrysostom, exhorted his flock of ordinary folks in this fourth-century homily:

I'm always encouraging you—and I'm not going to stop encouraging you!—to keep on reading sacred Scripture. And don't let anyone say to me silly, contemptible words such as—"I'm stuck at the courthouse all day." "I'm tied up with political affairs." "I'm in an apprenticeship program." "I've got a wife." "I'm raising kids." "I'm responsible for a household." "I'm a businessman. Reading the Bible isn't my thing."

What are you saying, man? It's not your business to pay attention to the Bible because you're distracted by thousands of concerns? Then Bible reading belongs especially to you. You're always standing in the line of battle, you're constantly being hit, so you need more medicine than other people. For not only does your wife irritate you, but your son annoys you, and a servant makes you lose your temper. An enemy schemes against you, a friend envies you, a neighbor insults you, a colleague trips you up. Often a lawsuit impends, poverty distresses, loss of possessions brings sorrow. At one moment success puffs you up; at another, failure deflates you.

How many powerful inducements to anger and anxiety, to discouragement and grief, to vanity and loss of sense surround us on every side! A thousand missiles rain down from every direction. And so we constantly need the whole range of equipment supplied by Scripture.

Making it real

"It is to be feared," J.I Packer suggests,
"that many today who profess to be
Christs never learn wisdom,
through failure to attend sufficiently
to God's written word....

How long is it since you
read right through the Bible?

Do you spend as much time
with the Bible each day as you do
even with the newspaper?

What fools some of us are!—
and we remain fools all our lives,
simply because we will not take the trouble
to do what has to be done to receive the
wisdom which is God's free gift."

Do Packer's remarks describe me?
How much time do I give to quietly
reading and thinking about Scripture?
Do I have my priorities straight?

Giving it to God

Oh, how I love your word!
It is my meditation all day long...
It is a lamp to my feet
and a light to my path

(see Psalm 119:97, 105).

Dear God,
may these words become true of me!

NOTES:

Whose Truth Is True?

*or this I was born, and for this I came into the world, to testify to the truth. Everyone who belongs to the truth listens to my voice.' Pilate asked him, 'What is truth?'" (John 18:37-38).*

Pilate's skeptical question to Jesus has a curiously 20th-century ring. I thought of it recently when an acquaintance told me she had resigned her position with a Christian organization because it required her to promote points of view that ran counter to Christ's teaching. Her protests had been met with the argument, "We can't be boxed into a narrow mentality that goes against what so many Americans are thinking today." Apparently in this case, keeping pace with secular culture was more important than being faithful to the word of God.

What is truth? Unfortunately, many Christians are just as confused as anyone else by the question. Too many of us have swallowed the lie that truth is debatable, subjective, determined by telephone surveys and celebrity interviews and public opinion polls. Is there life after death? Who is God? What's the purpose of life? Whose rules should govern areas like sexual morality and social justice? In our culture the answers to many such questions are usually seen as completely up to the individual: "It's whatever seems right to you." In many people's eyes, the most important thing is to be non-judgmental and accepting.

But Jesus didn't approach truth as a function of democratic consensus. He wasn't interested at all in getting everybody to agree on it and vote it in. He was interested in what he knew to be the will of God—both the almost unbelievably happy parts and the hard parts as well. Jesus was the incarnation of compassion, but He didn't try to make the truth easier to swallow by watering it down. The mercy He offers isn't for those who distort God's truth; His mercy is for those who take it seriously and turn to Him in repentance when they falter in living out its requirements.

Taking God seriously means rejecting the notion that truth is a theory or an interesting idea that we can alter at whim. "You cannot construct truth at all: you can only discover it," says Harry Blamires in his book *The Christian Mind*. "You do not make the truth. You reside in the truth." Believe me, I know how uncomfortable it can be to hold this position, to insist that truth is a matter of what God thinks, not what we think. Especially when it comes to the parts of God's word that don't seem fair or reasonable to our limited way of thinking.

Still, God is God. Truth is truth, whether I grasp it or not. I have to admit that my understanding can go only so far. So I make no apologies for the Gospel. And neither should you.

We have to insist that the Christian Faith is something solider, harder, and tougher than even Christians like to think. Christianity is not a nice comforting story that we make up as we go along, accommodating the demands of a harsh earthly reality with the solace of a cherished reverie. It is not a cosy day-dream manufactured by each person more or less to suit his own taste. It is a matter of hard fact. We Christians appreciate its hardness just as much as those outside the Church. We are as fully aware of its difficulties as the outsiders are. We know that, in a sense, Christianity leaves us with an awful lot to swallow. No Christian, thinking christianly, divesting himself of the easy self-deceptions of secularist thinking, will pretend that Christianity is an easy faith—easy to accept, easy to explore, easy to rest in, easy to explain. It isn't. We must outdo the unbelievers in agreeing with them on that subject. We must stand at their side and look with them at this thing, the Christian Faith, and vie with them in detaching ourselves from it. "You find it difficult? So do I. You find it awkward? So do I. You find it unattractive? That's exactly how I often find it myself, especially round about 7 o'clock on a Sunday morning. You think it a thundering nuisance? In a way I quite agree with you. It is a thundering nuisance at times, especially in Lent. But it's true, you know."

That's the point. It's true. The Christian mind is alive, quivering with the awareness that here is truth and all truth.

Harry Blamires

Making it real

If you had to participate in a debate about truth, would you choose to argue for or against the following assertion by Blamires. Why?

"Christian truth is objective,
four-square, unshakable.
It is not built of men's opinions.
It is not something fabricated either by
scholars or by men in the street,
still less something assembled
from a million answers,
Yes, No and Don't know, obtained from
a cross-section of the human race.
Christian truth is something given,
revealed, laid open to the eye of the
patient, self-forgetful inquirer."

On what occasions have you felt
that you could not say:
*I am not ashamed of the gospel;
it is the power of God for salvation
to everyone who has faith* ?

Romans 1:16

Why were you apologetic?

Giving it to God

To whom can I go, Lord?

You alone have the words of eternal life.
I will cling to your words,
even when public opinion
ridicules or rejects them.

NOTES:

Real Searchers Always Find

n some ways today the hostility toward certainty, clarity, and authority in connection with God's word is linked to an idolatry of "the search" or "the journey." Searching or journeying toward truth and meaning has been so elevated into a value, or assumed as our proper stance, that the very notion of finding truth that is clear, authoritative, and binding is consciously or unconsciously rejected or avoided.

During my undergraduate years as a student at the University of Notre Dame, and as a graduate student at Princeton, this love for the "search" was pervasive. For a period of time I rejected the teaching of Christ and the Church, and "searched" for truth. After a time, I came to realize that I often avoided those trains of thought or contact with certain people that would challenge or threaten my love of the "search." The prospect of finding or discovering truth threatened me. If I found the truth, I would have to submit to it. I saw that I had come to love the "search for truth" more than the truth itself. I had to repent of such idolatry in order to truly serve him who calls himself, quite simply and definitively, the Truth.

Indeed, an attitude which lies behind much of the attack on truth in the Church today is a growing doubt that human beings can know anything with clarity and certainty. Perpetual uncertainty is an intellectual posture quite congenial to contemporary, secular culture.

Ralph Martin

Jesus said, "Ask, and it will be given you; search, and you will find" (Matthew 7:7). I think that many people today never find out what life is all about because they never search in the proper places or end their search at the proper time. They surround themselves with noise and entertaining gadgets and ideas. They get too busy-busy, too caught up in the race for the kind of power, success, and wealth that society tells us is important. If they hear God's word, they never give it serious thought. Too distracted to look within, they miss God's invitation to become one with Him.

But it is not unusual these days to meet people who are missing the truth because they have chosen instead to be perpetual searchers—people who have gone from, say, a traditional Christian upbringing to hedonism to atheism and are now dabbling in Buddhism. To these hard-core seekers Jesus says, "Everyone who asks receives, and everyone who searches finds" (Matthew 7:8).

There is a time for searching, but there is a time for finding too. You can't keep your search going forever. If your search for truth is honest, at some point you realize that you know enough to be able to choose which master you will follow and serve. You may have questions; it may take some faith. Still, you have enough to go on. Prolong your search beyond this point and it becomes a pretext for maintaining your independence. This is the reality Ralph Martin faced up to: "The prospect of finding or discovering truth threatened me. If I found the truth, I would have to submit to it."

It seems to me that there is a third approach to the search for truth—the one adopted by the many people who go through the motions of Christian living without ever having submitted themselves to Christ. Seeming to have found the truth, they are clinging to their own way. Their Christian facade is just a defense against surrendering their personal "freedom."

What good does it do to try and look like a Christian if, in your heart, you refuse to submit to God's word? What does that yield? Jesus once rebuked a group of experts in the Jewish law for that same resistance: "You search the scriptures because you think that in them you have eternal life; and it is they that testify on my behalf. Yet you refuse to come to me to have life" (John 5:39-40).

However we may abandon or distort or neglect the search for truth, God doesn't stop searching for us. He calls us to meet Him, the living Word, in His word. There, as we give up our independent ways and pseudo-searching, He can give us the true freedom we crave: "If you continue in my word, you are truly my disciples; and you will know the truth, and the truth will make you free" (John 8:31-32).

Making it real

Have I ever seriously
searched for the truth?
With what results?

Where do I stand in my searching
at this point in my life?

Am I like any of the searchers
described here?

Giving it to God

O Lord,
you have searched me and known me.

You know when I sit down
and when I rise up;
you discern my thoughts from far away.

You search out my path
and my lying down,
and are acquainted with all my ways.

Even before a word is on my tongue,
O Lord, you know it completely....

Search me,
O God, and know my heart.

Psalm 139:1-4

NOTES:

Pitfalls of "Higher" Learning

here is heaven? One answer is that it's wherever God's Word is known and loved, proclaimed and obeyed. This means that heaven can be found here on earth, in some pretty unlikely-looking people and places!

Corrie ten Boom, who survived a Nazi concentration camp and told that story in the best-selling book *The Hiding Place*, traveled all over the world to share her experience and her faith. During a speaking tour in Korea, she met a theology student who was plunged in gloom because, as he told her, "I have lost my way and no longer know where heaven is." He explained: "When I first became a Christian, my pastor taught me the Bible is true. In those days I had great happiness. But now I am studying the famous scholar, Rudolph Bultmann, who says our Bible is full of myths and fables."

Corrie responded by recounting an experience that had reminded her of the reality and immediacy of heaven, as well as the reliability of God's word. Driving past a miserable shack in the countryside the day before, she had heard the voice of a woman singing. It was a concert hall-caliber voice, "like the song of a skylark."

I said to the missionary who was traveling with me, "Do you know that song?"

"Yes," she said, "it says, Where Jesus is, 'tis heaven there."

Oh, how my heart leaped for joy as I heard this beautiful song coming from such a poor place. It is one thing to hear such a song in a dignified church, or pouring through the speakers of an expensive stereo set. But when one hears it coming from the poorest shack in the midst of such poverty, then it means something else.

I looked at the young theological student before me. "Jesus said, 'The Kingdom of heaven is within you' (Luke 17:21). Bultmann is wrong and Jesus is right. Heaven is not a myth or fairy story. Heaven is a prepared place for prepared people. Theology in the hands of the Holy Spirit is a beautiful science. But in the hands of unbelievers it is death. If you want to find where heaven is, get out of your stuffy classroom and go back out into the countryside. Listen to the simple faith of those who read only the Bible and trust only in God, not in material things. What do they care if some theologian says that heaven is a fable. They have found Jesus, and where Jesus is, 'tis heaven there."

Corrie ten Boom

Jesus rejoiced in the Holy Spirit and thanked the Father for revealing the truth to the simple—to "infants" like the poor woman in Corrie's story—rather than to the "wise and the intelligent" (Luke 10:21).

There are, of course, many theologians and other educated people who perceive and accept the truth. But maybe those of us who have received a good deal of schooling encounter more roadblocks along the way to faith in God's word. Here are two of the obstacles that I think more educated people are prone to:

Intellectual arrogance. When higher education leads us to disbelieve and doubt God's word, it is really "lower" education. Who are we to set ourselves up as judges, "demythologizing" and reinterpreting whatever doesn't appeal to us? God's word judges us, not the other way around! Our little knowledge must always go hand-in-hand with reverent humility and fear of the Lord.

Passivity. A little knowledge can be deadening, as well as deceptive. For example, some people get so caught up in the literary beauty of the Bible, in its composition or history and social settings, that they never let it engage them personally. Some theorize about scriptural issues and meanings, but in an abstract way that never connects with real life. No sense of urgency accompanies their thinking, no feeling that something critical hangs in the balance and demands an immediate, profound response.

For all their knowledge, people who approach the Gospel like this are not taking God's word seriously. They never encounter Jesus in it. They never discover the important truth that is so obvious to more simple people: that "where Jesus is, 'tis heaven there."

Making it real

A theologian once remarked,
"To do theology, it is not enough
to know about God;
I must know God."

A similar point can be made
about studying God's word:
it is not enough to learn
about God in the Bible;
I must also be meeting Him in it.

In general, do you feel that you encounter
God when you read or hear Scripture?

Do you experience it as
a dead letter or a living Word?

Imagine your reaction if you knew that
Jesus was sitting in the next room
ready to lead you into His Word,
as he led the Emmaus-bound disciples
(see Luke 24:13-35).

Would you feel excitement?
Expectation? Awe? Openness?
Do you approach Scripture like this?

Giving it to God

Lord, open my mind to understand
Scripture and to receive it as one of the
simple ones who make you glad.

NOTES:

NOTES:

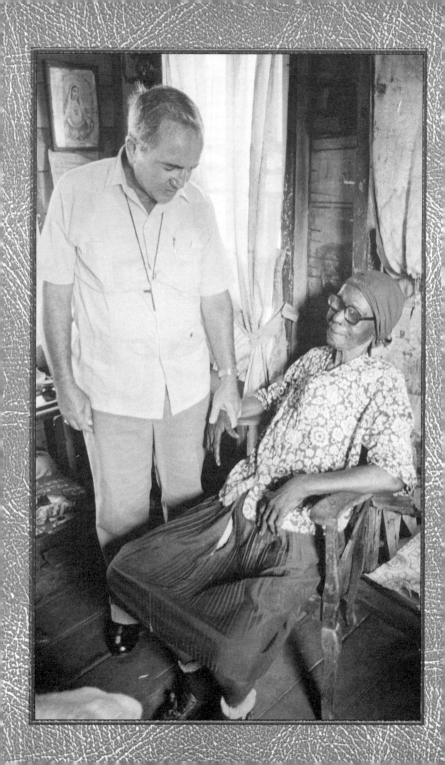

Doers Act, Hearers Forget

If any are hearers of the word and not doers,

they are like those who look at themselves in a mirror and,

on going away, immediately forget what they were like.

But those who look into the perfect law,

the law of liberty, and persevere ...

they will be blessed in their doing.

James 1:23-25

Choose Your Foundation!

*veryone then who hears these words of mine and acts on them will be like a wise man who built his house on rock. The rain fell, the floods came, and the winds blew and beat on that house, but it did not fall because it had been founded on rock. And everyone who hears these words of mine and does not act on them will be like a foolish man who built his house on sand.*

The rain fell, and the floods came, and the winds blew and beat against that house, and it fell—and great was its fall!

Matthew 7:24-27

Corona's house is falling down. Corona is 83 or so and lives alone in a decaying shack in Jamaica. Its rotting, termite-infested boards don't give her much protection when the winds blow and the rains fall. But Corona also has another house, one that's not visible to human eyes. That house is solid, a secure shelter against the ultimate loss and destruction that human beings most fear. Corona knows God and has built the house of her life on His word.

To take God's word seriously, it isn't enough to know it; like Corona, we must conform our lives to it. We must do it. Jesus made this very clear. "Not everyone who says to me, 'Lord, Lord,' will enter the kingdom of heaven, but only the one who does the will of my Father in heaven" (Matthew 7:21).

As with so many of the poor, Corona's difficulties have oriented her to approach God's word in a personal, earnest way. It's been a struggle. But how rich and secure Corona is, compared to the more materially well-off whose lives rest on the flimsy foundation of me, myself, and I!

An Italian sociologist quoted recently in the New York Times pointed to this poverty of the self-centered affluent: "Prosperity has strangled us," he said. "Comfort is now the only thing anybody believes in." And in the same article a 31-year-old biologist in Sweden commented, "We live in the richest place and at the best time, and everyone is wondering whether they can afford to take their next vacation or buy a boat. It's kind of sickening, really."

As I write this I'm conscious of the fact that I and most of my readers come from places that are relatively rich, compared to most of the world. Prosperity threatens to strangle us too. How can we resist the preoccupation with personal comfort which dulls our openness to God's word?

One vital factor is vigilance about engaging Scripture in a personal way. If, when I read the Bible, I don't have the sense that it's God's word for me right now, I won't take it to heart and apply it to my life. It's like seeing a "to do" note on the bulletin board or the kitchen counter: unless I know it's meant for me, I probably won't do what it says. Or, to use another image, if I don't know the check is in my name, I won't deposit it in my account.

For the Danish philosopher Soren Kierkegaard, reminding oneself to take Scripture personally was the key to taking it seriously: "When you are reading God's word you must continually say to yourself, 'It is talking to me. It is talking about me.'" Without this vigilance, he insisted, our instinct of self-protection will always find cunning and deceptive ways to avoid being arrested and converted by God's word.

Kierkegaard explained that in reading the parable of the Good Samaritan, a person must never assume a superior position and pass judgment on the priest and the Levite: "You shall not say: 'It is not I....'" No, when you read God's word, you shall be earnest and shall say to yourself, 'This priest is myself. How could I be so merciless and still call myself a Christian!'" Same story with the Levite: "Here you shall say: 'It is I. How could I be so hard-hearted! How could this happen again when it happened to me once before! How can it be that I have not become better!'" Kierkegaard allowed a relaxing of this vigilance only with regard to the Samaritan: "In order not to grow weary of incessantly saying, 'It is I,' you can here say for a change, 'It was not I; alas, no, I am not such a person!'"

Don't you think that if more of us read Scripture this way more often, the world would be a different place?

Making it real

Open your Bible to Luke 10:30,
and try reading the parable of the
Good Samaritan in the way Kierkegaard
suggests. Give it a good ten minutes.

— Start by asking the
Holy Spirit to help you.

— Read slowly,
putting yourself in the place of
each person in the parable,
one at a time. Picture the scene.
Use your imagination.
Keep reminding yourself:
This is talking to me!
This is talking about me!

— Listen.
Give the Lord a chance to speak to you.

— Ask yourself how to
put what you've learned into practice.
Decide on something specific to do today.

Giving it to God

Jesus, master builder!

Teach me to build my house
on the solid rock of your word.

NOTES:

Perfection for the Imperfect

ake time right now to read through the whole Sermon on the Mount. I guarantee that you'll be depressed. You'll say, "I couldn't ever, even if I lived a thousand years, possibly live up to this sermon."

Some Protestant writers, observes renowned Lutheran scholar Joachim Jeremias, have suggested that the Sermon on the Mount is so utterly unattainable precisely to convince us that it is impossible for us to be saved. In other words, Christ put these burdens on us and then said in effect, "Well, you can't do it. But now you know what it's like to be saved." It seems to me that such an interpretation falls short of the "good news" of salvation!

Doctor Jeremias points out that the good news of the gospel includes not only the moral teaching of Christ but also the proclamation that he is the Savior. This is a very crucial point, one which easily flies over our heads.

If Christ only preached the doctrine in the Sermon on the Mount without ever proclaiming himself to be the Savior of the world, says Dr. Jeremias, then we would indeed bear an impossible burden. But the gospel assures us that we cannot save ourselves. Even with the help of Christ, we are not our own saviors. Christ alone is the Savior of the world. He promises that his grace will well up inside us, that he can and will transform us and make us into what we are not.

Benedict J. Groeschel

When Scripture's call to perfection confronts our personal sin and weakness, as it does in the Sermon on the Mount (just read chapters five, six, and seven of Matthew's Gospel!), we are easily tempted to discouragement and depression. A foreboding feeling of failure undermines our openness to God's word and may even prevent us from ever trying to take it seriously. "I can't do this," we tell ourselves. "It's too much. After all, I'm only human." But this common complaint sells both God and ourselves short.

There's no getting around it: human beings are called to be perfect doers of God's word—and we are imperfect. But God has resolved this apparent contradiction. His saving power at work in us transforms us; it makes us perfect by uniting us with Himself.

So what's our part in the process? Surely, we don't get to just sit by and watch while Jesus builds our house on the rock! Otherwise, why would He have warned us to put his words into practice?

C.S. Lewis says that our part is like playing a game of "let's pretend." Not hypocrisy, where you try to appear as something you're not, but the good kind of pretending, "where the pretence leads up to the real thing." Love your enemies, seek first the kingdom of God, have no anxiety—when you encounter situations that call for biblical, beyond-your-strength responses like these, you try to act as you know you should. Even though you don't feel able or inclined to do it, you take a step in faith and "put on the Lord Jesus Christ" (Romans 13:14). As you do, Lewis says, Christ himself "is actually at your side and is already at that moment beginning to turn your pretence into a reality."

If you've been taking God's word seriously, I'm sure you've noticed this dynamic many times in your own life. For me, one small example concerns how Jesus helped me reach out in love to people with leprosy and AIDS. On my first visits to leprosariums and homes for the dying in Haiti, I shrank from touching anyone. I knew this wasn't very loving, but the sight of so many bodies so ravaged by these terrible diseases left me shaken and fearful of contracting them myself.

"Jesus," I prayed one day, "I know you want me to love these sick people as you have loved me. Please help me to express your love by touching them." It wasn't easy to shake hands with the next leprosy patient I encountered, but that was the turning point. Hugs and handshakes have not been a problem for me since.

Truly, God makes his grace well up inside us when we ask him to help us do his word. As Benedict Groeschel says, "He can and will transform us and make us into what we are not.

Making it real

Have you ever felt depressed
by God's call to perfection?

Do you tend to take sole responsibility
for the job of making yourself holy?

What's wrong with that approach?

Can you think of any instances when
you knew what God wanted you to do,
felt you couldn't do it,
but relied on God and tried anyway?
What happened?

Giving it to God

Lord, when I get depressed
about how imperfect I am,
help me remember
what You said to Paul:
*"My grace is sufficient for you,
for my power is made perfect
in weakness."*

And help me to respond, like Paul:
*I will boast all the more gladly
of my weakenesses,
so that the power of Christ
may dwell in me.
For whenever
I am weak,
then I am strong!*

(see 2 Corinthians 12:9, 10).

NOTES:

Francis of Assisi:
Daring to Look Foolish

hen on a certain day the Gospel was read in the church—about how the Lord sent his disciples out to preach—Francis, the holy man of God who was assisting there, understood only some-what the words of the Gospel. After Mass he humbly asked the priest to explain the Gospel to him more fully. The priest set forth in order all these things for Francis: how the disciples of Christ should not possess gold or silver or money; nor carry along the way scrip, or wallet, or bread, or a staff; that they should not have shoes or two tunics; but that they should preach the kingdom of God and penance. Hearing this, the holy Francis immediately cried out exultingly: "This is what I wish, this is what I seek, this is what I long to do with all my heart."

Then the holy father Francis, overflowing with joy, hastened to fulfill that salutary word he had heard, and he did not suffer any delay to intervene before beginning devoutly to perform it. He immediately put off his shoes from his feet, put aside the staff from his hands, was content with one tunic, and exchanged his leather girdle for a small cord.... He was not a deaf hearer of the Gospel, but committing all that he had heard to praiseworthy memory, he tried diligently to carry it out to the letter.

Thomas of Celano

People who take God's word seriously come to it with the attitude, "Speak, Lord, for your servant is listening" (1 Samuel 3:9). They listen attentively, they hear, and then, as faithful servants, they obey.

Francis of Assisi had already given himself radically to God before the incident described above took place. But he always kept looking for ways to follow God more closely. Thomas of Celano, his contemporary and first biographer, describes here how Francis discovered God's personal word of direction in Matthew 10:7-10. Francis jumped to obey it, traveling light as he preached the Gospel throughout central Italy. Later, when other men joined him, this text became the basis for their way of life.

Ever since Jesus invited two fishermen to follow him, men and women throughout history have kept responding to his call. A well-known modern example comes from the life of Mother Teresa of Calcutta. On September 10, 1946, as she traveled to Darjeeling on a night train crowded with poor people, she pondered Matthew 25:40: "as you did it to one of the least of these you did it to me." Through this verse she heard Christ inviting her to a new mission of service to the poorest of the poor.

In a similar way, reflecting on the parable of the rich man and Lazarus (see Luke 16:19-31) drew Albert Schweitzer to become a doctor in order to relieve the suffering of the people of French Equatorial Africa. He abandoned the comforts of Europe and a distinguished career in music and theology and spent half a century serving the sick at his jungle clinic.

Francis, Mother Teresa, and Albert Schweitzer were each judged foolish and imprudent by some of the people around them. For Francis, at least, the accusation may sometimes have been justified. But as one writer has suggested, isn't there a lesson for us even in his possible excess of zeal?

St. Francis of Assisi has become one of our most loved saints. He has enchanted us with his simplicity, his charity toward the poor, his fellowship with all God's creatures. However, we seem to avert our eyes from his extremism— his forsaking all for the gospel, his embracing poverty, his obeying Scripture literally. We would be better Christians if looking at Francis's extreme side caused us to respond to God with a more robust faith and to obey his word more closely.

The wisdom of the cross is foolishness in the eyes of the world. Following the Gospel means having to take some stands that go against the flow. That threatens people. So if you and I take a serious approach to living by Jesus' words, then eventually we're going to be criticized too. It's inevitable.

Consider the opposition and hostility that Jesus provoked, even from within His own family. How can we expect universal approval, if it is His word we are trying to live by? And if we never meet with criticism, whose word are we living by anyway?

Making it real

Can I think of other examples of men and
women who were so struck by God's word
that it changed the way they lived?
Do I know any of them?
What does their example say to me?

Does God's word have a practical
effect on how I live and think?
Do any examples, big or small,
come to mind?

Which extreme do I most
need to guard against:
being excessively careful and concerned
about looking foolish to others,
or being rash and unnecessarily offensive?

Giving it to God

Almighty, eternal, just and merciful God,
grant us in our misery and grace
to do for you alone what
we know you want us to do,
and always to want what pleases you.

Francis of Assisi

NOTES:

A Word for the West

f I had to say where I think the word of God sounds most challenging to First World ears, I'd probably pick out what it teaches about the concern that Christians are to have for the poor. Because this teaching threatens to change our use of time and money, as well as the ideals of affluence we absorb from countless media images, we shy away from its implications. But we can hardly take God's word seriously if we gloss over those parts which especially confront our society's status quo!

This is an immense subject with many angles. Here are a just a few thoughts to stimulate your own reflections.

God has a special concern for the poor. This concern is evident throughout the Old and New Testaments. We should prick up our ears at the biblical warnings that idolatry, affluence, and oppression of the poor will provoke God's judgment.

The Old Testament prophets, for example, declared that injustice against the poor is a crime against God. They denounced as empty formalism the religious actions offered by the mercilessly rich and powerful. Don't come to God with "burnt offerings" and "thousands of rams, with ten thousand rivers of oil," Micah warned: "What does the Lord require of you but to do justice, and to love kindness, and to walk humbly with your God?" (Micah 6:8). Forget the sackcloth and ashes if you're oppressing the needy, said Isaiah. Offer instead the kind of fasting God wants: loose the bonds of injustice, free the oppressed, feed the hungry, shelter the homeless, cover the naked, satisfy the needs of the afflicted (see Isaiah 58:3-10).

God identifies with the poor. Jesus, God's most perfect revelation of himself, did not cling to His divine prerogatives when He came among us. He "emptied himself, taking the form of a slave" (Philippians 2:7). He grew up in a poor family, in a country that was under foreign domination. He spent most of His earthly life in the cultural and economic backwater of Galilee, from a town so undistinguished that even a fellow Galilean could sneer, "Can anything good come out of Nazareth?" (John 1:46). He launched His public ministry by announcing that He had come to fulfill God's promise of good news for the poor, release to captives, healing for the sick. To the hungry He offered miraculously multiplied bread. He identified himself so closely with the needy that He said that He himself was the recipient of merciful actions extended to the suffering (see Matthew 25:31-46).

God calls us to share His concern for the poor. Scripture is emphatic on this point. In fact, Ronald J. Sider wonders, in his book *Rich Christians in an Age of Hunger,* can we call ourselves Christians if we neglect it?

To those who do not feed the hungry, clothe the naked, and visit the prisoners, Jesus will speak a terrifying word at the final judgment: "Depart from me, you cursed, into the eternal fire prepared for the devil and his angels" (Matthew 25:41). The meaning is clear and unambiguous. Jesus intends that his disciples imitate his own special concern for the poor and needy. Those who disobey will experience eternal damnation.

Lest we forget the warning, God repeats it in 1 John 3:17-18. "But if any one has the world's goods and sees his brother in need, yet closes his heart against him, how does God's love abide in him? Little children, let us not love in word or speech but in deed and in truth." (See also James 2:14-17.) Again the words are plain. What do they mean for Western Christians who demand increasing affluence each year while Christians in the Third World suffer malnutrition, deformed bodies and brains—even starvation? The text clearly says that if we fail to aid the needy, we do not have God's love—no matter what we may say. It is deeds that count, not pious phrases and saintly speeches. Regardless of what we do or say at 11:00 A.M. Sunday morning, affluent people who neglect the poor are not the people of God.

Ronald J. Sider

This can sound like a harsh judgment, but Sider qualifies it by also stating his conviction that millions of Christians in affluent lands care about Jesus more than anything else and will "take any risk, make any sacrifice, forsake any treasure, if they see that God's word demands it." That's what I think too. If it weren't for such people, Food For the Poor couldn't exist.

But first we must become aware of the need and the call to share our resources with the poor. We must examine our conscience often. Then, prodded out of our comfortable cocoons, we can truly be doers and not just hearers of this countercultural word.

Making it real

Here is something to reflect on in examining your approach to the poor. It comes from a biblical and liturgical commentary that I have read daily for the last 25 years. Read it and then talk it over with the Lord.

Should fidelity to the gospel entail the voluntary reunuciation of money? Not all can follow this vocation. But all should be concerned that they be not slaves to riches, that they should use their possessions (material and other) in the service of humanity. There is no doubt that we face urgent and concrete demands in this way by virtue of the sort of poverty we do profess. Today it can be said that, by and large, Christians are better off materially than the majority of human beings. It may be that in these circumstances the Spirit is urging voluntary poverty on a wider scale. Aware of the prophetic import of this, it remains for each one of us to examine his conscience.

Thierry Maertens and Jean Frisque

NOTES:

NOTES:

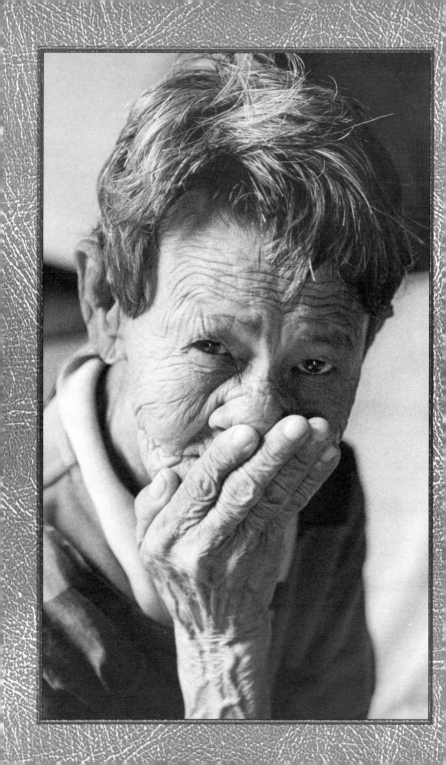

Getting Serious

The abbot Moses asked the abbot Silvanus, saying,

"Can a man every day make a beginning of the good life?"

The abbot Silvanus answered him,

"If he be diligent,

he can every day and every hour

begin the good life anew."

Sayings of the Desert Fathers

When Shall I Begin?

 ery truly I tell you, when you were younger, you used to fasten your own belt and go wherever you wished. But when you grow old, you will stretch out your hands, and someone else will fasten a belt around you and take you where you do not wish to go." (He said this to indicate the kind of death by which he would glorify God). After this he said to him, "Follow me."

Peter turned and saw the disciple whom Jesus loved following them; he was the one who had reclined next to Jesus at the supper and had said, "Lord, who is it that is going to betray you?" When Peter saw him, he said to Jesus, "Lord, what about him?" Jesus said to him, "If it is my will that he remain until I come, what is that to you? Follow me!"

John 21:18-22

Everybody seeks happiness. Everybody wants to know what life is all about. Jesus is the answer to our searching. He said, "I am the way, and the truth, and the life. I came that they might have life, and have it abundantly" (John 14:6; 10:10). But not everybody is ready to act on Jesus' words once they learn what it takes.

For the rich young man who came to Jesus asking what to do, the answer was more than he had bargained for. He couldn't bring himself to accept Jesus' invitation, "Come, follow me" (Mark 10:21). In refusing it, he missed his chance to discover life's real purpose and deepest joy.

Why does Jesus invite us to follow him? Because He wants to share his life with us! He wants to bring us into union with Him; He wants to introduce us into the very heart of the love that exists among Father, Son, and Holy Spirit. Union with God is what life is all about. And saying yes to it is the key to happiness; it enables us to start enjoying heaven's abundant life right here on earth.

God's word sets before us a wide range of possible responses to Jesus' summons. There is the rich young man, who says no regretfully, knowing he is missing something. There is Nicodemus, who comes to Jesus in secret, for fear of what his own colleagues might think. There is Judas, who goes back on his initial "yes," betrays Jesus, and then dies in despair. There is Peter, who also denies Jesus but accepts the grace of a fresh start. And there is the beloved disciple, as well as many others like him who accept Jesus' invitation without hesitation—Zacchaeus, Matthew, Mary Magdalene, and the other women who followed Jesus…

If we read about these people's choices in a detached way, we are missing the point. The very same choice confronts us. It's no one-time decision either. Again and again through the changing circumstances of our lives, we must answer Jesus' question: Will you follow me? Will you let me lead you, even when the road is one you'd rather not travel—when it takes you where you do not wish to go? Will you come?

Don't gauge your response by what you see other people doing. This matter is between you and God. And don't think that if you've been shrugging it off or responding half-heartedly, you no longer have the capacity to make a wholehearted response. What matters right now is not the fact that you may have said no to Jesus initially or somewhere along the line; what matters is what you say today! As one devotional book put it, "What matters is not our first reaction to God's call, but the courage not to justify our own unwillingness."

I read once about a very saintly man who died in his eighties after a lifetime of intimacy with God and heroic love of God and neighbor. During his last years he often exclaimed, "When shall I begin to do good?"

No matter where we're at in our Christian life, it seems to me we could all stand to ask ourselves the same question from time to time. "When shall I begin to do good? When shall I begin to take God seriously?"

With God helping, we will seize the grace of the present moment to return his love and serve him wholeheartedly today…and then tomorrow…and the next day.

Making it real

If you had lived in Jesus' day
and had heard him speak,
how do you think you would
have responded to him?

What makes you think that?
Do you suppose it would have been
harder or easier to say yes to him?

Choose two or three Gospel
passages where Jesus is inviting
someone to "come, follow me."
Using the Scripture-reading guidelines
on page 92, insert yourself into the story
and imagine your response.

Giving it to God

Dear Lord Jesus…

I am still so divided.
I truly want to follow you,
but I also want to follow my own desires
and lend an ear to the voices that speak
about prestige, success, human respect,
pleasure, power, and influence.

Help me to become deaf to these voices and
more attentive to your voice, which calls me
to choose the narrow road to life.

Henri J. M. Nouwen

NOTES:

Destination: Holiness

I f my religion is only a formal compliance with those modes of worship that are in fashion where I live; if it costs me no pains or trouble; if it lays me under no rules and restraints; if I have no careful thoughts and sober reflections about it, is it not great weakness to think that I am striving to enter in at the strait gate?

If I am seeking everything that can delight my senses and regale my appetites; spending my time and fortune in pleasures, in diversions, and worldly enjoyments; a stranger to watchings, fastings, prayers, and mortification; how can it be said that I am working out my salvation with fear and trembling?... If I use the world and worldly enjoyments as the generality of people now do, and in all ages have done, why should I think that I am amongst those few who are walking in the narrow way to heaven?...

We cannot offer to God the service of angels; we cannot obey Him as man in a state of perfection could; but fallen men can do their best, and this is the perfection that is required of us...

The best way for anyone to know how much he ought to aspire after holiness is to consider not how much will make his present life easy, but to ask himself how much he thinks will make him easy at the hour of death.

William Law

How could any book about taking God seriously not contain an excerpt from William Law's *A Serious Call to a Devout and Holy Life*? Written in 1728, this spiritual classic still speaks forcefully to us about the importance of understanding and pursuing God's call to holiness.

It isn't that our own efforts make us holy: God is the one who sanctifies. Yet holiness won't just "happen" to us unless we seek it, embrace it and live it.

Driving in and out of the church parking lot every Sunday won't make us holy. Following Jesus in a way that our society finds acceptable won't make us holy. Unless we are seeking after Jesus aggressively every day, we are not responding to Jesus' call, "Come, follow me." We are not really taking God seriously. We haven't yet grasped what life is all about.

Too many of us assume that we should leave holiness to the saints and the religious professionals. "Not for me," we decide. "I'm just an ordinary person living an ordinary life." What William Law would tell us is that we're setting our sights way too low!

When Jesus said, "Follow me," He excluded no one. In the Gospels we meet many of the ordinary, imperfect, average men and women who first responded to Jesus. He called them all to become holy as God is holy.

There are not two tracks in the Christian life, one for "gifted" and another for "average" disciples. Christ calls all of us without exception to the fullness of loving union: "If we love one another, God lives in us, and his love is perfected in us" (1 John 4:12).

The perfection of love—it's important to realize that this is what we're agreeing to when we travel the path of discipleship. Perfection comes at a price: the crucifixion of our ego. If we set out on the journey without understanding this, we will most likely turn back when things start getting uncomfortable.

C.S. Lewis speculates that many of us find ourselves good enough Christians long before God does. Having overcome a sin or two, he says, "We should be obliged if He would now leave us alone. As we say, 'I never expected to be a saint, I only wanted to be a decent, ordinary chap.'"

What about you? Are you convinced that God is calling you to be holy? Are you taking Him up on the invitation? Will you let Him bring you beyond being "decent" and "ordinary"—to the level of perfect love?

Making it real

Someone once commented
that on their deathbed,
no one ever wishes they had
spent more time at the office!

If I followed Law's suggestion
and thought about what would
make me "easy" at the hour of death,
what would that be?
How would it make a difference
in the way I live today?

Seriously now, do I want to be holy?
Am I truly prepared to let God do whatever
it takes to bring me to perfect love?

Talking to God

Have your way with me, Lord.
Fill me with your love.

Make me a channel of
your perfect love
to everyone I meet.

Notes:

Making God Number One

oliness consists of carrying out God's will with joy. Faithfulness forges saints.

Spiritual life is union with Jesus—the divine and the human in mutual giving. The only thing Jesus asks is that I commit myself to him, in total poverty, in total forgetfulness of self.

The first step toward holiness is the will to attain it. With a will that is whole we love God, we opt for him, we run toward him, we reach him, we possess him. Often, under the pretext of humility, of confidence, of abandonment, we forget about using our will. But it all depends on these words—I want or I do not want. I have to pour all my energy into the words I want.

We cannot decide to become saints without a great effort of renunciation, of resisting temptations, of combat, of persecution, and of all sorts of sacrifices. It is not possible to love God except at one's own expense.

Mother Teresa

Mother Teresa of Calcutta was a tiny, unprepossessing woman with a somewhat meek demeanor. When it came to following Jesus and serving him in the poor, though, she was like a pit bull: she never let go.

I know a woman in Jamaica who has this same determined spirit. She's a single mother who lives in a shack on a garbage dump with her many children and an aged parent. Beverley is one of those desperately poor people who turn to God quite naturally while they are very young. After her first two children were born, though, she abandoned God. Ten hard years later she made up her mind to repent. "Running, running I came back to Jesus," she says. "Nothing would trip me up this time, nothing would take me away from him." And nothing has. "Living holy to almighty God" is Beverley's daily goal.

This is the kind of resolve you and I need if our journey to God is to continue and bear fruit. We must decide to make God our first priority. We must take a hard look at everything in our life—choices, values, relationships, lifestyle, and so on—and reassess it all in light of the Gospel. Making God number one must become our number one concern, our passion and motivation.

It's like marriage. If I'm married, I must place my relationship with my spouse above every other human relationship. After God, my spouse must have first claim on my heart. Otherwise our marriage is headed for trouble.

I don't think we put enough emphasis on the importance of choosing God above all else. Some of us have never really thought about it. Many of us live with divided minds, sort of wanting God, but wanting other things too. "A sickness of the mind," Saint Augustine called this partial willing and partial non-willing.

"Choose life," Moses told the people of Israel. Choose to live "loving the Lord your God, obeying him, and holding fast to him" (Deuteronomy 30:19-20). "Choose me," Jesus tells us. "Put me first every day. I am the way and the truth and the life. You won't regret it."

Once we've chosen Jesus, we must find concrete ways to express our choice in the way we live. Otherwise it's just a mind game. Now I'm not suggesting that God wants you to move into the shack next door to Beverley. But He does expect your daily schedule to reflect your new priorities.

My own post-conversion scheduling decisions included time for silent prayer and attending the liturgy every day. I also decided to educate myself spiritually by reading good books about the Christian life. (That's how I encountered many of the authors I'm sharing with you in this series.) Time for serving the poor also became a priority.

Giving some time to God in ways like this helps us to consecrate all our time to God. By reminding us of the main purpose of our existence, it helps us to view the whole day differently and offer all our activities to God.

"Whatever you do, do everything for the glory of God," Saint Paul advised (1 Corinthians 10:31). If we make a firm decision for God, this will become our way of life too. What cosmic consequences hang on those little words, "I want" and "I do not want"!

Making it real

In general, have I been
loving God at my expense,
or loving myself at God's expense?

Could anyone who didn't know me
tell from the way I live that
I am a follower of Christ?

"I have to pour all my energy into the
words *I want*," Mother Teresa said.

Ask yourself: what do I want?
Take some time to brainstorm about
how to pour your energy into loving God.
Write down as many practical
suggestions as you can think of.
Choose one to implement today.

Talking to God

Jesus,
I believe that you are the way,
the truth,
and the life.

I choose you.
Help me to pour
all my energy
into wanting you.

NOTES:

The Deadliest Choice

sense of deep sadness comes over me when I think of how Christians sit on the fence. What is the matter with us? Have we forgotten that we are followers of a crucified Christ? Have we forgotten that he was just the son of a carpenter, himself a tradesman, a strange itinerant preacher who crisscrossed the tiny country of Palestine, preaching his gospel to the poor? Have we forgotten that following him means to take the greatest risk that man can take? Have we forgotten that following him means living dangerously?

It seems that we have spent centuries trying to eliminate the risk and the danger of his call. It seems that we have cushioned the risk and practically eliminated any and all danger by drawing up a set of moral rules that give us security instead of holy insecurity; rules that lull our conscience to sleep instead of making it wide awake and ready to undertake the risks of being a Christian.

Christ said that if we are not with him we are against him. How do we measure up to this saying of his? Are we really with him? Are we ready to give up father, mother, sister and brother, in the sense he means it, that following him demands? Are we ready to lay our lives on the line of his law of love with its fantastic dimensions of dispossession and surrender? Do we truly love one another, beginning with ourselves?

I wonder how long we can sit on the fence of compromise. God is not mocked!

Catherine Doherty

Why did I wait until I was in my forties to start taking God seriously? Why did it take an unusual encounter with God to focus my attention on the way I was living? When I stop and think about it, I come up with these main reasons. Maybe you can relate to them.

❖ Lack of understanding. Although I had been raised in a religious family, it never dawned on me that the purpose of my existence was union with God. God and I were separate entities, I thought. Someday I would die and travel to the great beyond and He would reward me for following a few rules. Meanwhile, God was distant, my conscience was lulled to sleep as Catherine Doherty describes, and I basically did my own thing.

❖ Preoccupation with the material world. My pursuit of success and wealth was relentless, but it never involved assessing what true success and wealth might be. I worked hard to provide my family and myself with every material comfort—without considering what might bring me comfort in the life to come! "Dispossession and surrender" were the last things on my mind.

❖ Self-centeredness. In both my business and my personal life, I was driven by the desire for power and control. Forget the "holy insecurity" of following Christ! I was captain of my ship and I sailed wherever I wished. I sought my pleasure above all things, setting my own rules and investing significant time and money in recreational diversions.

❖ Busyness. Driven by my goals and desires, I was constantly on the move. One reason I never thought about what I was living for was that I gave myself no time for quiet reflection. Maybe I was afraid to.

Catherine Doherty talks about sitting on the fence of compromise. Fence-sitting implies that a person has not yet made the choice to reject God. In some ways that was true of me: I had never consciously rejected God. But you can also say that fence-sitting itself is a choice: not to choose Jesus wholeheartedly is to decide against him. That's what Jesus himself said: "Whoever is not with me is against me" (Matthew 12:30).

Fence-sitting is a deadly choice, because indifference to God involves sloth, a cold sin that is harder to overcome than outright rebellion. "God can more easily cool our wrath than fire our frozenness, though he can do both," observes philosopher Peter Kreeft. And why is sloth so dangerous? Kreeft explains:

Sloth simply does not play God's game, either with him or against him. It sits on the sidelines bored while life and death are at stake. Out with it! Better be God's enemy than a clod. Better be either hot or cold than lukewarm. If that seems harsh, it is God's word, not mine, and he used an even more unflattering expression than "clod" in Revelation 3:16: "vomit."

Not to "play God's game, either with him or against him" is really a choice. It's a decision not to take God seriously, which is an option for hell. So don't be deceived! This is no spectator sport. It's the only game in town, and the stakes are unimaginably high.

Making it real

Look over the four excuses for
putting God off that are listed above.
Can you relate to any of them?
What would you add?
Ask yourself:
Am I responding to God
as seriously as I can right now?

Why are "cold" sins like sloth,
indifference, lukewarmness, and
ingratitude so dangerous?
Am I rejecting God's love
in any of these ways?

Christ said that if
we are not with him
we are against him.
How do I measure up to this saying?
Am I really with Jesus
and ready to undertake the
risks of serious discipleship?

Giving it to God

Jesus, I love you.

I will follow you.

Do with me what you will.

NOTES:

What Happened to the Rich Young Man?

I keep thinking about that rich young man. Jesus looked at him and "loved him" before giving him the invitation to "come, follow me." How different his life would have been if he had taken that look and that call seriously. He might have become one of the Lord's closest followers, another "beloved disciple." He would certainly have led a richer, more meaningful life.

Every day Jesus is looking at us as He looked at the rich young man: with love. Every day He is calling us to put aside our games and our attachments to whatever keeps us from being serious about God. Every day He invites us to surrender fully to Him. Unlike the rich young man, we still have time to make or renew our decision to say "yes" to Jesus' loving invitation.

In my opinion, this often avoided, misunderstood and underestimated choice to take God seriously is the most profound, emotional, and energizing event a Christian can experience. It is the ultimate turning point, the crossroads at which we choose the wide, easy path or the narrow, rough way to life (Matthew 7:13). It is the eternal marriage commitment we make with the divine bridegroom, Jesus Christ.

Does the decision leave you breathless? It should. Has the thought of following Jesus ever impacted you this way before? Why not?

When the rich young man was faced with the choice of following the Lord, I believe he understood the awesome importance of his decision — perhaps better than many of us do today. Ironically, what he may not have fully grasped was the great prize Christ was also offering to him. For the rich young man, saying "yes" only meant losing everything. He never seemed to see the wonderful opportunity Jesus' call represented. If the young man had taken these blessings as seriously as he took the challenges of following Jesus, perhaps his response would have been different.

If this book serves no other purpose, I hope and pray it encourages you to reflect on your own understanding of God, His love, His call to surrender and service, His blessings — everything. Taking God seriously is not an answer, it is an approach to life and to the whole Christian experience.

In the years ahead, I hope to continue this series by introducing and reflecting upon other, more specific fruits of our faith, including the freedom of surrender, the joy of trust and the power of prayer. Through these and other blessings, God reveals that He is serious about us!

Sources:

INTRODUCTION: THE MYTH OF "MINIMUM REQUIREMENTS" CHRISTIANITY

viii   C.S. Lewis, *Mere Christianity*. New York: Macmillan Publishing Company, 1960, p. 175

ONE: GAMES CHRISTIANS PLAY

3   Jean Vanier, *Be Not Afraid*. New York: Paulist Press, 1975, p. 107.

6   Thomas Merton, *Thoughts in Solitude*. New York: Farrar, Straus & Cudahy, 1958, p. 34.

11,12   Dietrich Bonhoeffer, *The Cost of Discipleship*. New York: The Macmillan Company, 1973, pp. 88, 90.

13   Helmut Thielicke, *The Waiting Father*, trans. John W. Doberstein. New York: Harper & Row, 1959, p. 150.

15   *God Is No Stranger*, Prayers of Haitian Christians, ed. Sandra L. Burdick, trans. Eleanor Turnbull. Rockford, Michigan: Baptist Haiti Mission, 1987.

17,18   Augustine of Hippo, *The Confessions*, trans. Maria Boulding, O.S.B. Hyde Park, New York: New City Press, 1997, pp. 198, 204-5, 262.

23   Francis de Sales, *Introduction to the Devout Life*, trans. John K. Ryan. New York: Doubleday/Image, 1989, pp. 39-40.

TWO: A GOD THAT ISN'T GOD

34   Dionysius the Areopagite. Quoted in *The Soul
       Afire*, ed. H.A. Reinhold. New York:
       Doubleday/Image, 1973, p. 46.
34   J.B. Phillips, *Your God Is Too Small*. New York:
       The Macmillan Company, 1954, pp. v, 63.
40   Hannah Whitall Smith, *The Christian's Secret of a
       Happy Life*. Uhrichsville, Ohio: Barbour
       Publishing, pp. 49-51.
41, 42 J.B. Phillips, *Your God Is Too Small*, pp. 128-9.
45, 46 Thomas Merton, *Conjectures of a Guilty
       Bystander*. New York: Doubleday/Image, 1989,
       pp. 127, 128.
47   Charles Colson, *Against the Night*. Ann Arbor,
       Michigan: Servant Publications, 1989, p. 103.
47   Philip Yancey, *The Jesus I Never Knew*. Grand
       Rapids, Michigan: Zondervan Publishing
       House, 1995, p. 114.
51, 52 Carlo Carretto, *The God Who Comes*, trans. Rose
       Mary Hancock. Maryknoll, New York: Orbis
       Books, 1974, pp. 207, 208, 209.
53   *Catechism of the Catholic Church* for the United
       States of America, United States Catholic
       Conference, Inc./Libreria Editrice Vaticana,
       1994, par. 399.

THREE: WORDS OF LIFE AND TRUTH

59   John Chrysostom, "Seven Homilies on
     Lazarus," homily 3, in J.P. Migne, *Patrologiae
     Graecae*, vol. 48, Paris, 1862, col. 993. Trans.
     K.F. Perrotta.

62   J.I. Packer, *Knowing God*. Downers Grove,
     Illinois: InterVarsity Press, 1979, p. 104.

62   John Chrysostom, homily 3 "on Lazarus,"
     cols. 991-93.

64   *Knowing God*, p. 91.

69   Harry Blamires, *The Christian Mind*. Ann Arbor,
     Michigan: Servant Books, 1978, p. 113, 112.

70   *The Christian Mind*, p. 120.

70   *The Christian Mind*, p. 113.

73, 74   Ralph Martin, *A Crisis of Truth*. Ann Arbor,
     Michigan: Servant Books, 1982, pp. 29-30.

79, 80   Corrie ten Boom, *Tramp for the Lord*, with Jamie
     Buckingham. Fort Washington, Pennsylvania:
     Christian Literature Crusade; Old Tappan, New
     Jersey: Fleming H. Revell Company, 1974,
     pp. 134-5.

FOUR: DOERS ACT, HEARERS FORGET

90   Michael Specter, "Population Implosion
     Worries a Graying Europe," *The New York Times*
     (July 10, 1998)

91   Soren Kierkagaard, *For Self-Examination*.
     Minneapolis: Augsburg Publishing House,
     1940, p. 51.

92   *For Self-Examination*, pp. 46-47.

95   Benedict J. Groeschel, C.F.R., *Heaven in Our Hands*. Ann Arbor, Michigan: Servant Publications, 1994. p. 33. Joachim Jeremias comments in *The Sermon on the Mount*. Philadelphia: Fortress, 1963, pp. 34-35.

96   C.S. Lewis, *Mere Christianity*, pp. 161, 162.

101   Thomas of Celano, *St. Francis of Assisi*, trans. Placid Hermann, O.F.M. Chicago: Franciscan Herald Press, 1962, pp. 22-3.

103   Bert Ghezzi, *God's Word Today* (December 1996), p. 17.

108   Ronald J. Sider, *Rich Christians in an Age of Hunger*. Downers Grove, Illinois: Intervarsity Press, 1978, p. 82.

109   *Rich Christians*, p. 58.

111   Thierry Maertens and Jean Frisque, *Guide for the Christian Assembly*, vol. V, trans. Molaise Meehan, O.S.B. Notre Dame: Fides/Claretian, 1972, p. 266.

FIVE: GETTING SERIOUS

115   *The Desert Fathers*, trans. Helen Waddell. New York: Henry Holt and Company, 1936, p. 149.

121   Henri J. M. Nouwen, *The Road to Daybreak*. New York: Doubleday, 1988, p. 137

123,124 William Law, *A Serious Call to a Devout and Holy Life*. Philadelphia: The Westminster Press, 1948, pp. 22, 23, 25.

125   C.S. Lewis, *Mere Christianity*, p. 173.

129   Mother Teresa, *Heart of Joy*. Ann Arbor,
       Michigan: Servant Books, 1987, p. 92.

135   Catherine de Hueck Doherty, *The Gospel
       Without Compromise*. Notre Dame, Indiana: Ave
       Maria Press, 1977, pp. 74-5.

137   Peter Kreeft, *Back to Virtue*. San Francisco:
       Ignatius Press, 1992, pp. 154-5.

BIOGRAPHICAL NOTES:

AUGUSTINE OF HIPPO (354-430) was born in North Africa of a pagan father and a devout Christian mother. Educated as a Christian, he deviated into years of loose living and heresy before returning to the faith at 33. Nine years later he became bishop of Hippo. The best-known writings of this great Western Church Father are his autobiographical *Confessions* and his 22-volume *City of God*.

HARRY BLAMIRES studied literature at Oxford under the tutorship of C.S. Lewis and, at his encouragement, began writing works of theology and philosophy in addition to literary criticism. His insistence on the revealed, absolute nature of Christian truth earned him a chilly reception in British theological circles, especially during the period when a "demythologizing" approach to Scripture was in vogue.

DIETRICH BONHOEFFER (1906-1945), German Lutheran pastor and theologian, was alert to the threat of Nazism from the very beginning and fought it by joining the resistance movement. Arrested for helping to smuggle Jews out of the country, he spent two years in prisons and concentration camps before finally being hanged at Flossenburg in 1945. He is known especially for *The Cost of Discipleship* and *Letters and Papers from Prison*.

CARLO CARRETTO (1910-1988) was an energetic leader
of a dynamic Catholic youth movement in Italy when
he heard God's summons to a life of contemplative
prayer. Leaving everything behind, he set out for
Algeria and the Saharan desert, where he joined a
religious order called the Little Brothers of Jesus.
Among the dozen popular books which flowed out of
this new life are *Letters from the Desert* and *The God
Who Comes.*

FRANCIS DE SALES (1567-1622), Catholic bishop of
Geneva and Doctor of Church, was a renowned
spiritual writer and counselor. His insistence that
spiritual perfection is possible for every Christian, not
just religious "professionals," is one of the main
themes of his timeless *Introduction to the Devout Life.*

CATHERINE DOHERTY (1896-1985), a Russian who fled
her homeland and emigrated to Canada after the
Communist Revolution, abandoned a promising career
in response to Christ's invitation to "sell all, give it to
the poor, follow me." Moving into the slums, she
served the needs of the poor by establishing
"Friendship House" centers in places like Toronto,
Chicago, and Harlem. Today hundreds of men and
women follow her example of prayer and outreach to
the needy by participating in Madonna House
Apostolate, based in Combermère, Ontario.

FRANCIS OF ASSISI (1181-1226), party-loving son of a
wealthy merchant, became the talk of Assisi when, in
the town square, he dramatically renounced his
inheritance to serve Christ in the poor and embrace
"Lady Poverty." His simple life of itinerant preaching,

prayer, and works of mercy attracted a band of followers which developed painfully into a religious order. Francis is especially remembered for his burning love of God and the poor, his life of simplicity, and his love of God's creation.

BENEDICT J. GROESCHEL, a Capuchin Franciscan Friar, is the Director of Spiritual Development for the Catholic archdiocese of New York, a psychologist, spiritual writer, and founder of a religious order. His books, tapes, and TV presentations address today's spiritual needs by using selected insights from modern psychology to explore aspects of the Christian life. *Spiritual Passages, Arise from Darkness,* and *Stumbling Blocks and Stepping Stones* are a few of his many books.

WILLIAM LAW (1686-1761) was educated and ordained an Anglican deacon at Emmanuel College, Cambridge. Dismissed for refusing the Oath of Allegiance to King George I, he served as tutor in a prominent family for ten years before finally being ordained to the priesthood. The last 20 years of his life were devoted to prayer, works of mercy, and writing. His book *A Serious Call to a Devout and Holy Life* has deservedly become a classic of spiritual literature.

RALPH MARTIN rethought and rejected his faith while attending a Catholic university, becoming an outspoken critic of the church and an admirer of thinkers like the "death of God" philosopher Nietzsche. In 1964, at a friend's insistence, he attended a Christian retreat; there he encountered the Lord and returned to his faith with enthusiasm. Involved in many evangelistic projects since then, he currently heads Renewal Ministries and hosts a weekly television program, *The Choices We Face.*

THOMAS MERTON (1915-1968) became an instant celebrity with the 1948 publication of *The Seven Storey Mountain,* his account of his conversion to Catholicism and entrance into the Trappist abbey in Gethsemane, Kentucky. A prolific writer on many topics—prayer, social responsibility, violence, Eastern spirituality—he is generally considered the most influential spokesman of our day for traditional monasticism. Among his other best-selling works: *The Sign of Jonas, Thoughts in Solitude, No Man Is an Island, New Seeds of Contemplation,* and *Conjectures of a Guilty Bystander.*

MOTHER TERESA (1910-1997) was born in Skopje, Yugoslavia, into a close-knit and religious Albanian family. At eighteen she left home forever, first to train as a Sister of Loreto in Dublin, then to teach at a girls' school in Calcutta. Eighteen years later, after hearing Jesus' call to live and serve among the "poorest of the poor," she left her convent to begin the work for which she is now universally recognized.

RONALD J. SIDER, a historian and professor of theology at Eastern Baptist Seminary, angered and unsettled many readers with his 1977 surprise best-seller, *Rich Christians in an Age of Hunger.* Especially jarring was his "bringing sin into the language of world poverty," as one journalist described it. Faulted for sometimes simplistic solutions and a strident tone, Sider is nonetheless seen as serving an important conscious-ness-raising function—"part of the yeast and salt of American Christianity." Among his other books: *Cry Justice*, *Living More Simply*, and *Cup of Water, Bread of Life*.

CORRIE TEN BOOM (1892-1983) spent her first 50 years living a quiet, devoutly Christian life with her father and sister in Haarlem, Holland. During the Nazi occupation, the trio opened the family home as a hiding place for persecuted Jews until, betrayed by an informer, they were arrested and sent to concentration camps; only Corrie survived. Following her release, she became an indefatigable traveler for Jesus, sharing with audiences in more than 60 countries her conviction that "there is no pit so deep that Jesus is not deeper still."

HANNAH WHITALL SMITH (1832-1911) was born into a strict Quaker home in Philadelphia. After a long period of deep doubt, she experienced a spiritual renewal and with her husband became a popular Bible conference leader for many years. Personal tragedy led her to the understanding of suffering and obedience presented in many of her 19 books, the best-known of which is *The Christian's Secret of a Happy Life*.

About Food For The Poor:

Food For The Poor is an interdenominational, nonprofit charitable organization that began in 1982 as Ferdinand Mahfood's attempt to take seriously the words of Jesus: "I was hungry and you gave me food, thirsty and you gave me something to drink, a stranger and you welcomed me, naked and you gave me clothing, sick and you took care of me, in prison and you visited me" (Matthew 25:35-36).

Now a lifeline to thousands in the Third World, Food For The Poor channels its funds, goods, and services through clergy, missionaries, and others who are already working with the poor on-site. "We simply ask, 'What do you need?' and then supply whatever is requested," Mahfood explains. "This hands-on approach makes it possible to respond to real needs in the most direct and speedy way possible."

Food For The Poor has mushroomed since the days when Mahfood would hand out a few bags of rice to priests and pastors in Jamaica and Haiti. From 1982 to 1998, more than $433 million worth of food, medicine, housing materials, and other aid has gone out to the poorest of the poor in the Caribbean and Latin America.

As new needs emerge and requests for help multiply, Food For The Poor aims to keep growing in its ability to respond. "So far, we've never had to refuse a legitimate request," says Mahfood. "We'd like to keep it that way!" Anyone interested in serving Jesus in the poor by helping to meet this goal can contact Food For The Poor at:

Food For The Poor, Inc.
550 SW 12th Avenue
Deerfield Beach, FL 33442
(954) 427-2222
www.foodforthepoor.org

To make a donation or receive an information package:
(800) 282-POOR

"Every contribution is important, no matter how small," says Mahfood, as he thinks back to his first modest efforts to serve the poor. "If we take God seriously and offer what we can, He will take us seriously too. He will give us to others in ways far beyond anything we could have imagined. That's the story of Food For The Poor."